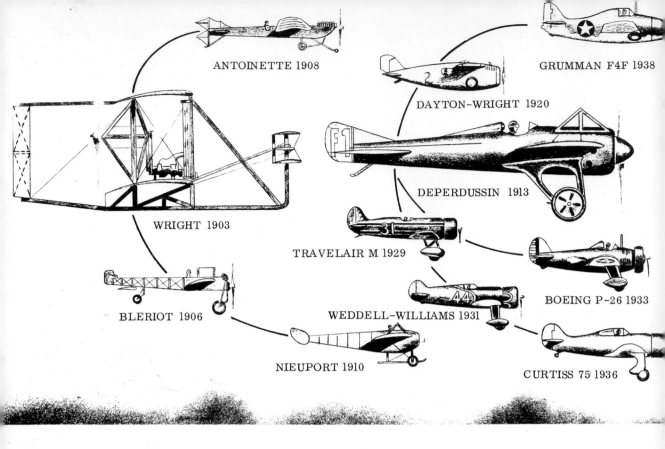

ANTOINETTE 1908

GRUMMAN F4F 1938

DAYTON-WRIGHT 1920

WRIGHT 1903

DEPERDUSSIN 1913

TRAVELAIR M 1929

BOEING P-26 1933

BLERIOT 1906

WEDDELL-WILLIAMS 1931

NIEUPORT 1910

CURTISS 75 1936

"*Instead of the tardy conveyance of ships and chariots, man might use the swifter migration of wings, the fields of air are open to knowledge and only ignorance and idleness need crawl upon the ground.*"

—Rasselas, DR. SAMUEL JOHNSON, *1759*

Written and Illustrated by Reed Kinert

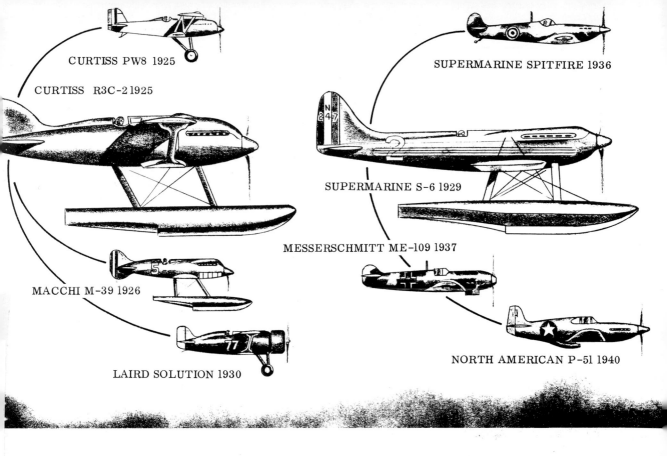

CURTISS PW8 1925

CURTISS R3C-2 1925

SUPERMARINE SPITFIRE 1936

SUPERMARINE S-6 1929

MESSERSCHMITT ME-109 1937

MACCHI M-39 1926

LAIRD SOLUTION 1930

NORTH AMERICAN P-51 1940

RACING-PLANES

and air races

A Complete History

VOLUME I
1909-1923

AERO PUBLISHERS, INC.

Fallbrook, California

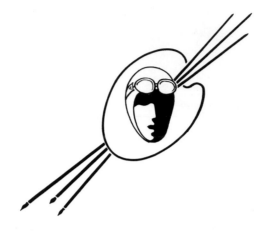

DEDICATION

To the designers, builders, and pilots of racing air-
craft, for their contribution to the science of flight.
and
To my patient wife Eleanor who typed the text three
times!

FIRST EDITION

LIBRARY OF CONGRESS CATALOG CARD NUMBER
67-16455

Foreword

As a small boy I watched my first air race, if it could be called that — a race between an automobile and an airplane. The automobile won, at 40 miles an hour.

Since that day, closed-course racing speeds of airplanes have exceeded 600 miles per hour. The history of air racing — the events which made possible this tremendous advance during my lifetime — is the chronological record of the sacrifice and accomplishment of the men and women who made this history. Some of them you will meet in this book. Many others, however, are anonymous heroes: unfamiliar by name, known only through their work.

It is difficult for me to think of air racing as a sporting event. Men, not machines, indulge in sports. But to me, air racing is a contest between machines. It implies a conquest of speed, rather than a contest in speed.

The contest between men in air racing is largely the matching of wits in the design and building of the airplane and in its preparation for the race. Although I am sure that some will challenge my opinion, I feel that the pilot of a racing plane is not really the contestant. What he does or does not do has very little effect on the outcome of the race, provided, of course, that he uses everyday piloting skill and techniques and that he follows prescribed racing procedure. The two most perfect performances of race flying I can recall watching, one by a man and one by a woman, illustrate this point. In the case of the man, it was the first closed-course race he had ever flown; in the case of the woman, it was the first time she had ever touched the controls of a purely racing plane. They both won their races — because the planes were right!

I have found that if the flight characteristics of a racing airplane are tricky enough to require more than average skill in a race, it is very unlikely that it will ever be a winner. It certainly will never be a consistent one. Below-par design just can't be offset by above-par piloting.

The racecourse is a stern taskmaster for the airplane. It makes the pilot pay a high price for small deficiencies in original design or for laxity or incompetence in preparing the plane for the race. It is equally cruel and unforgiving of mistakes made by the pilot during the race.

The men and women who made air-racing history have been driven by an urge far more compelling than any instinct relating to sport, pleasure, or self-advancement. Yet it is hard to define this urge. I have been asked on many occasions, "What good is air racing? What has it done for aviation?" I find it difficult to answer specifically, for the benefits are numerous and varied. In groping for the answer, I find many more intangibles than tangibles and feel strongly that the intangibles are far more important.

The tangibles are more or less limited to the sort of thing that auto racing has done for the development of the automobile. The economic necessity or urge to "win" has in many instances prompted important developments in aircraft design considerably earlier than would have occurred in ordinary progress.

One intangible result of air racing, which indicates the gruelling tests imposed by the racecourse, occurred in the Jet Thompson Trophy Race of 1949. This was a race between three F-86's, our current high-speed fighters. These planes had passed all the stringent tests imposed on our Air Force jet fighters, but they found the racecourse still more exacting. All three planes suffered serious structural failure before the race was finished. The design corrections that resulted from these failures helped our flyers in Korean skies.

The intangible benefits of air racing are numerous. The chief one is that interest in air racing stimulates young people into technical study and eventually into the design and building of aircraft. Racing planes offer the best opportunity for designers to test their ideas and ingenuity. Usually only one racing plane of each design is built, and for that reason the hundred-odd racing planes built in this country in the four years for the Goodyear and Continental Trophy races alone represent a greater number of original and complete designs than has been produced by the entire aircraft industry in the same period. Less than a year after it was announced that races would be held for a new classification of "midget" airplane, thirteen new racers had been designed, built, tested, and raced.

This performance by the back-yard designers presents a real challenge to our great aircraft industry. The time factor in their accomplishments is particularly significant when you consider the accepted interval of several years between the time an airplane is designed and the day it can be flown away from the factory. In spite of the hundreds of millions of dollars spent on new aircraft designs following the attack on Pearl Harbor, only one, a Grumman F6F Hellcat, was ready for use in World War II. All the other planes used in that war were already in production or had entered the blueprint stage before Pearl Harbor.

From a monetary angle, I think that the achievements of these back-yard designers should provoke a complete analysis of the methods used by the engineering departments of large aircraft manufacturers, considering that dozens of original back-yard racers can be designed, engineered, built, and tested to exacting requirements for less than the cost of a *single* wind-tunnel model recently used by one of our large organizations as an aid in the design of a new aircraft!

In preparing this book, Reed Kinert has done aviation people the world over a real service. The accuracy and detail in which this exciting phase of the history of aviation is covered bespeaks much painstaking research.

It will be a treasured addition to my library as a reference aid from a technical standpoint, and as an aid to reminiscing. I will be reminded of many events, both happy and sad, of fine men I've raced against who are no longer here to read this, and of other fine men I've raced against who have since earned the gratitude of a nation for a different kind of flying. All have done their part in the advancement of aviation.

Ben O. Howard

Benjamin O. Howard
Consulting Engineer
Consolidated-Vultee Aircraft
Fairchild Aircraft Corp.

AUTHOR'S NOTE

From the beginning of air racing in 1909 to the last pre-World War II races of 1939 the development of racing planes and their engines contributed directly to the technology applied to aircraft built in assembly-line quantity, both military and commercial craft.

Having wondered for years when and where air racing began I went, one foggy morning while awaiting take-off from the local bean patch, to yon library for a bit of research.

Many libraries, hundreds of letters and thousands of books and magazines later I had to publish—in an effort to repay myself the time and effort spent!

Actually it has been fun. I have treasured letters in my files from famous, near-famous and unsung designers, builders, and pilots the world over. And many good friendships were made in my quest for the ever elusive last word or photograph of a particular aircraft or event.

Being a long time admirer of artist Clayton Knight, and reminful of how nicely his sketches dressed up so many aviation stories of WWI, I spent many hours on my drawing board embellishing the written word with action art, in hopes it would lend interest.

Dustin Carter, a fine scale drawing craftsman, has helped greatly to add book interest and the photo credits in our book are just that—in almost direct proportion to the number of photographs.

In these pages we depict but a few "stock" aircraft, military or civilian craft that, by having a number painted on, became racing planes. Rather we will use the valuable space to show, whenever possible, more than one view of each purely racing aircraft. When a particular production military or civilian aircraft was either extremely modified or as stock in appearance, did set a noteworthy record or win an important race we try to show that aircraft.

As I said—it has been fun and we hope you like it!

Reed Kinert

Reed C. Kinert
Commercial Pilot
No. 27006

Table of Contents

List of Illustrations

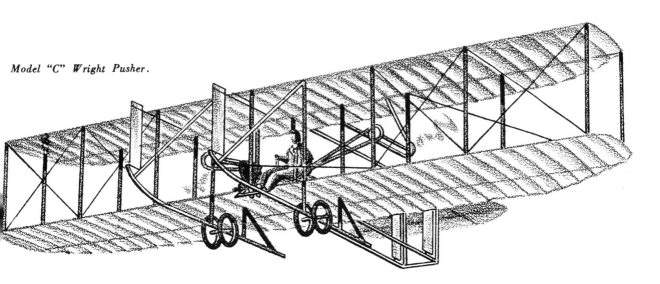

Model "C" Wright Pusher.

1909 – The First International Air Meet

News of Orville Wright's first engine-driven flight at Kitty Hawk, N. C., Dec. 17, 1903, and the several flights made afterwards by both Orville and Wilbur, had traveled around the world, mostly in disbelief. Then on Sept. 26, 1905, Orville made the first officially recorded flight, when he flew 11.12 miles in 18 minutes, 9 seconds, at Dayton, Ohio. Disbelief changed to amazed wonder.

In France, Aug. 22, 1906, Brazilian-born Alberto Santos-Dumont made the first recorded European flight—in a boxkite-like biplane. The continental designers Leon Delegrange, and the brothers Farman and Voisin followed Santos-Dumont with their biplane aircraft in quick order. Bleriot in that same eventful year of 1906 had built and flown the world's first successful powered monoplane. Glenn Curtiss, like the Wright brothers, had manufactured bicycles, and followed the Wrights in the United States by building his biplane *June Bug* complete to its engine. He flew it June 21, 1908. The astonishing progress of aviation was on.

The newly formed Aero Clubs of France, England, and the United States soon decided to gather all the aviation clan together, realizing the tremendous boost it would give the newly born science, from both a public and an engineering viewpoint. Their plans culminated in 1909.

Just six years after the Wrights had made their powered flights, the first International Air Meet of heavier-than-air machines took place near the old cathedral town of Rheims, France, on the field of Bethany, where the troops of Joan of Arc had once camped.

Held August 22–29, the International races attracted over 100,000 people daily. The ancient little city seethed with excitement. A small hotel suite was $500 for the week, and the tiniest of rooms $10 a day. Dozens of special trains ran from Paris, and Paris itself was crowded by fans who worshiped their favorite flyers more fervently than movie stars are worshiped today.

Louis Bleriot, who had earlier that year been the first to fly the English Channel, and who was acknowledged the greatest flyer in France, was at Rheims with five machines of his own design. One, especially built for the feature speed event, the Bennett Cup race, was a big monoplane with a V-8 60-hp E.N.V. engine.

Hubert Latham's hangar held two Antoinettes, with widespread wings and pointed noses, powered by new Antoinette V-8 engines which delivered 50 hp. These aircraft were designed by Leon Levavasseur, designer of the Antoinette motorboats, and the nose of his aircraft looked much like a boat's prow. Even at this early date, streamlining appeared; the Antoinette was an example, with its sleek boatlike fuselage and copper tubing running along the fuselage sides for cooling the engine water.

In another hangar was young Bunau-Varilla's new Voisin, which looked like an oversize box kite. It had no ailerons; only the enclosed ends of the wings and the vertical planes between them gave it lateral stability, leaving it impossible to bank or maneuver properly in turns.

In the same hangar was Louis Paulhan's Voisin, powered by a 7-cyl. Gnome rotary motor, in which

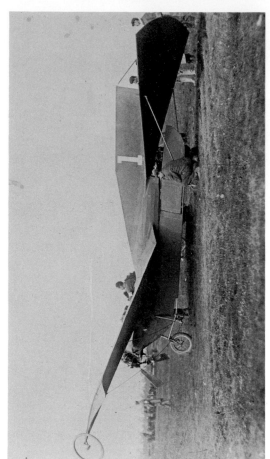

At rest on one of its wing tip outrigger wheels the R.E.P. looked like a crackup but was an unusually clean aircraft except for its excessive tail surface. It was flown in the meet by its designer-builder, M. Robert Esnault-Pelterie.
(Musée de l'Air)

Louis Bleriot awaiting a crank after tinkering with the engine in his Bleriot XII built especially for Rheims. Fabric is removed from wing trailing edge to gain access to wing warping mechanism which Bleriot used instead of ailerons.
(Musée de l'Air)

The Antoinette No. 13 flown in 3rd place in the Bennett by Hubert Latham was, with its dragonfly grace, reminiful of a Jules Verne dream come to life. Its configuration proved to be years ahead of both Bleriot and Curtiss.
(Musée de l'Air)

Wright Model C, one of three appearing at Rheims. Seen rounding the home pylon it was flown to 4th place by Eugene Lefebvre of France. The Wright brothers were still launching aircraft by catapulting from wooden monorails, then landing on skids.
(Musée de l'Air)

Remarkably sharp photo of a Curtiss Model D, for which the Golden Flyer became a prototype, taking off at Hammondsport, N.Y., in 1911. Photo reveals, more than any other we have located, the rickety bamboo construction and single-surface fabric covering typical of all early Curtiss aircraft. The only visible difference between this Model D and the Rheims Flyer is the absence of a fabric covered vertical stabilizer in and above the front elevators. Model D also carried a larger rudder. (Curtiss)

the whole engine revolved with the propeller around the crankshaft. This ensured fine air-cooling of the cylinders, but the efficiency loss in spinning the engine was great.

Tissandier, de Lambert, and Lefebvre were there with Wright machines. Lefebvre's, a cut-down model built in France, was faster than the conventional Wright. All three of these machines had the advantage of not having to drag a landing gear through the air, as they were still launched from monorail trolleys, as the first Wright plane had been; they landed on their curved wooden runners.

The hangar of the French constructors Henri and Maurice Farman held two enormous biplanes. Their wing span stretched clear across the hangar. A single surface elevator jutted high out in front of the wings, while the broad boxed tail extended far rearward. The landing gear was a massive structure of struts and skids, which supported two pairs of wheels slung on thick rubber shock bands. The huge Farmans were powered by Gnome rotary engines; only 35 hp to drive that mass of wood, fabric, and wire through the air! They might fly a long time but certainly not very speedily.

Glenn Curtiss was the lone American entry, sponsored at the last moment by Courtlandt Bishop, President of the Aero Club of America. The Wrights had declined to enter, for they regarded themselves as scientists, ready for any risk essential to their experiments but not for mere glory. Curtiss knew that he was second choice, and had accepted only because he

sorely needed the possible prize money with which to continue his plane building.

Glenn's machine was the smallest there, a pusher biplane with but a 26-ft. wing span. The wings were covered with linen fabric and doped with a yellowish varnish which gave the plane a golden appearance and its name—*Golden Flyer.*

Curtiss had designed the 50-hp engine, his most powerful one to date. It was a V-8 water-cooled type and turned a 7-ft. propeller.

The most unique aircraft of the meet were three R.E.P. monoplanes, designed and built, complete to 35-hp radial engines, by M. Robert Esnault-Pelterie. The fuselage and wing were built up with steel tubing, the wing was full cantilever, there were no brace wires or struts showing on the aircraft, the propeller was 4-bladed, and the landing gear was bicycle type. Only their low-powered engines kept these R.E.P. planes from the winning ranks.

The Rheims meeting was a great success. There were prizes for time and distance covered, one for altitude, and a daily contest for speed (the *Tour de Piste*) flown over a 10-km course (6.21 miles). A balloon anchored in the center of the airdrome enabled spectators to judge the altitude of the contestants.

Hubert Latham (who later met his death while hunting big game in Africa) took the altitude prize and the world's record by ascending to the then terrific height of 503 feet. This was as daring a performance as any at the meet. Almost any of the machines present was capable of going higher, and many of them later ascended several thousand feet. It was the men themselves who were incapable of attaining altitude. They were still earthbound, venturing but a little way into the atmosphere, exploring it almost foot by foot. To them, flying high seemed not safer, as we now know it to be, but incredibly dangerous. Safety belts had not been thought of as yet, and who of us today would fly one of those crates in rough or even in smooth air, to any height, *with* a safety belt!

The planes were underpowered, unstable, many with no ailerons or other form of lateral control, with balky engines and novice pilots—yet how they flew! Thrill after thrill brought the spectators to their feet as records fell in rapid succession. Here was flying such as the world had dreamed of but had never seen before.

On the first day, despite a muddy field, six planes were in the air at once for the first time in history. As they landed, six more took their place. There were 38 "ships" at Rheims, and 36 of them actually flew.

The air was rough through most of the race meet —at one time 12 crashed aircraft lay scattered around the airdrome in mute warning. There were no deaths, for the machines were slow and the crash impact was lessened by the crumpling of the lightly constructed wood-and-fabric craft. Accidents seemed to spur the pilots on to further achievement and increased the admiration of the crowd.

Latham flew in heavy rain and nonchalantly rolled cigarettes in flight. Bunau-Varilla delighted the crowd by politely tipping his hat each time he flew by the grandstands. Fournier and Tissandier enthusiastically participated in every event, though they won none. The dirigibles, *Colonel Renard* and *Zodiac III*, droned across the sky and demonstrated to many the superiority of the airship over the airplane.

August 27 was the last day of competition for the time-distance race. Paulhan had bested the Wrights' incredible record of 124 km (77.04 miles) in 2 hrs. 20 min. 23 sec., made at Le Mans, France, in December 1908, and Latham had beaten that. Paulhan covered 134 km (83.26 miles) in 2 hrs. 43 min., and Latham did 159 km (99 miles) in 2 hrs. 13 min. At 4:25 the last afternoon H. Farman dragged his heavy plane into the air in quest of the record. Latham, Delegrange, Lefebvre, and others were aloft and after the record, too. Long after all the others had landed, Farman's huge machine rumbled on around the course into the dark of night. When he landed, he had won the contest, setting a new world's time-distance record of 3 hrs. 4 min. 56.4 sec., and 118.5 miles. Sitting on the front of his plane at 40 mph for three hours had made Farman so cold and stiff that he was virtually congealed. He could not walk, and a big fireman carried him to the warmth and gaiety of the celebration in his hangar.

Throughout the race meet Curtiss and Bleriot had seesawed in winning the daily *Tour de Piste* for best speed, one lap around the 10-km course. Then on August 28 came the major speed event, the Bennett Cup race, which caused great excitement. The contestants were to fly the course separately and against time, two laps around the 10-km course. First prize was $5,000 and a magnificent silver trophy, presented by Mr. James Gordon Bennett as a companion prize to his already famous Bennett Cup for an annual free-balloon race.

That morning Curtiss took off to try his engine first in the daily 1-lap speed race. He climbed into the hot, still, and cloudless sky hoping for a smooth flight. But he quickly found that the air was literally boiling; the little plane bucked and pitched like a wild bronco. Fighting the controls, Curtiss tried vainly to find a reason for this turbulence. No one knew as yet that air becomes a series of up and down drafts caused by absorption of the sun's heat by dark objects on the earth's surface and a reflection of the heat by lighter objects.

Curtiss landed to see the record signal flying and learned that he had bettered Bleriot's best time by nine seconds. Although exhausted by his rough flight, Curtiss reasoned that the weather would get no better and could change to the rains that had so hampered the first days of the meet, so decided to try at once for the Bennett Cup.

Roaring across the starting line at 45 feet, with his engine held wide open for the first time, the plane bounced so hard that Curtiss was flung from his seat. Having no safety belt, he grimly hooked his feet in the frame, flew the two laps at an average speed of 47.7 mph, and landed after a diving finish with the record signal again flying.

Hundreds of people dashed across the field to congratulate him, and to them Curtiss stated, "It's my opinion that the turbulent air helped me. It probably broke up the partial vacuum, which, forming behind the plane, holds it back." Such was the theory of flight in those days!

Cockburn of England, in his huge bumbling Farman, followed Curtiss into the air. Then in order came Lefebvre in a Wright, Latham in an Antoinette, and Bleriot in his own machine. Bleriot soon outsped the rest and in the first lap equalled Curtiss' best, but his speed fell off in the second lap. Curtiss had won over Bleriot by 5.4 seconds. The Gordon Bennett Cup now belonged to the United States, where it would be contested for one year hence.

Wing tenders duck under lower wing panels and the American Flag flutters behind the front elevator to act as a drift indicator as Curtiss makes his start in the daily Tour de Piste on August 26th. Glenn wore no goggles at Rheims, had ten hours' total flight time and none on the Golden Flyer when he arrived at Rheims. (Musée de l'Air)

Bleriot's Rheims Racer XLL was a rather large monoplane, as evidenced by the men standing by. The large wood-laminated, four-bladed propeller was tried by Bleriot before the race but was replaced by its original two-bladed prop for the race. Bleriot sat in shade under the wing directly in back of the noisy, oil-spewing hot engine, complete with blast from the chain-driven prop. (U.S. Air Force)

Hubert Latham on his Antoinette

1910 – James Gordon Bennett Cup Race

Born in America, aviation developed fastest in Europe, with France soon taking the lead. She wanted the Bennett Cup regained by her airmen, or at least by her aircraft, and so she was well represented at the 1910 meet. Just after the 1909 Bennett race, Bleriot had bettered Curtiss' time by seconds, setting a new record of 47.8 mph. Orders for Bleriot planes increased steadily, and he wanted this happy condition to continue.

The 1910 International Air Meet and return engagement for the Gordon Bennett Cup was held in October at Belmont Park (N.Y.) Race Track, where the world's finest thoroughbred horses still to this day are running at their 30-mph pace. Most of the world's great airmen were there, and again prizes were offered for duration, distance, speed, and altitude. Orville Wright demonstrated his new Baby Wright racer and was timed unofficially at 70 mph, his engine not wide open. Roland Garros, by then perhaps the most daring if not the most skillful of foreign pilots, gave startling exhibitions in a Demoiselle monoplane designed by Santos-Dumont. Capable of 51 mph, the plane had its engine mounted on the wing, and the pilot sat below on the landing gear. With characteristic generosity, Santos-Dumont gave the drawings of the plane to anyone who wished to duplicate his handy, well-performing craft.

Genial, smiling Captain Baldwin, balloonist, dirigible pilot, parachute jumper, and tightwire walker, who learned to fly heavier-than-air craft at the age of 60 years—first man to fly across the Mississippi River and first man to sell parachute-jumping altitude by the foot, his rate being one dollar per foot and altitude starting at 2,000 feet—waited until the wind died down at sunset to pilot his tricky, all-steel *Red Devil*, also called the *Tin Goose*, through the skies.

Hoxley and Johnstone, nicknamed "The Heavenly Twins," flying after the altitude record, encountered a wind so severe that it swept them tail first across the heavens, forcing them to land many miles away from Belmont. Before the meeting ended, Johnstone, a former trick bicycle rider in vaudeville, had climbed to the undreamed of altitude of 9,714 feet.

Glenn Curtiss had built a fast new monoplane for the Bennett race, but was not sponsored by the Aero Club of America because of what they considered his stupid insistence on exhibition flying. They did not realize the financial necessity, plus the advertising value, that drove Curtiss to this distasteful task.

Eight pilots competed in the Gordon Bennett race on Saturday, Oct. 29. Claude Grahame-White of England was first away on his Bleriot. He flew the required 20 laps of the 3.1-mi. course in 1 hr. 1 min. 4.47 sec., averaging 61 mph for the 62 miles. The development of aircraft during the preceding year was clearly indicated by the greatly increased distance over last year's race.

Leblanc of France was next off on his Bleriot at a fast rate. For 19 laps he bettered Grahame-White's time, setting a new world's speed record of 71 mph on one lap. Then suddenly his machine seemed to go out of control on a low pylon turn and flew head-on into a telegraph pole, completely demolishing the Bleriot. Leblanc was lucky enough to escape with severe contusions and three bad scratches across the face.

Ogilvie of England, flying a C-type Wright, tried next, and though he completed the course later, he was forced down for 54 minutes owing to ignition trouble. (The rules permitted only one try for the Cup by each pilot.) Deducting the delay time, his speed was 51.6 mph, a remarkable performance bearing in mind that his machine was fitted only with the ordi-

Claude Grahame-White finishing the course in his Bleriot. He won the 1910 Bennett race with an average speed of 61 mph. On the ground are Brookins' Baby Wright racer (foreground) and the Curtiss racer which did not race.

15

nary 35-hp Wright engine. Ogilvie's total time for the 62.1 miles was 2 hrs. 6 min. 36 sec. for an official speed of 29.4 mph.

Brookins of the United States was up next, in the fastest entry of the race, the Baby Wright racer. But on the very first lap, while passing in front of the grandstand at 200 feet, the engine stopped cold. Brookins was slow to drop the nose to maintain flying speed, the racer stalled and dropped like a dead duck in full view of the horrified crowd, and rolled up the homestretch with its tail wrapped around its wings. When the dust blew away, Brookins was miraculously intact but severely bruised.

Hubert Latham of France, on his mahogany-colored Antoinette, also completed the full course but made one very long stop because of engine trouble. His total time was 5 hrs. 48 min. 53 sec. J. Radley, third pilot of the British team, made his try but soon landed his Bleriot when the 14-cyl. Gnome rotary engine failed.

Just before the deadline ending the 7-hour period during which competitors could start for the prize,

U. S. pilots Moisant and Drexel, both on Bleriots, started off in a last attempt to keep the Cup in America. Drexel was forced down after 7 laps. Moisant, however, completed the full course in the slow time of 1 hr. 57 min. and 44.85 sec., averaging 31.5 mph, thus securing second place in the races, Ogilvie taking third. By virtue of Grahame-White's victory, the Cup passed to England, and the next competition for it would take place there.

Seeing and hearing of the first International Air Meet to be held in the United States gave aviation here the impetus it needed. The Curtiss and Wright companies took many an order, as did Bleriot, who sold manufacturing rights to companies in England and the United States on a royalty basis. The U. S. Army and Navy, after viewing what was then an enormous increase in the speed-distance of the Bennett race, the new altitude record, and the general reliability of the aircraft, were influenced no little into expanding their viewpoint toward the airplane, and experts were predicting speeds of up to 100 mph!

◆ ◆ ◆

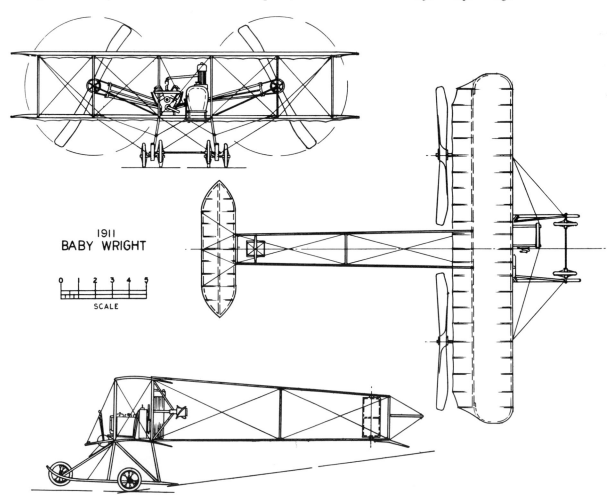

1911
BABY WRIGHT

SCALE

D.W. CARTER 10/66

1911–James Gordon Bennett Cup Race

By early 1911 over 1,000 aeroplanes had been successfully built and flown, covering a total distance of 150,000 miles. Bleriot alone had sold over 300 of his machines, which were in great demand because of their simplicity and fine showing at the race meets. Another French engineer, M. Nieuport, had studied Bleriot's monoplanes and compared them with biplanes. He was quick to see that the monoplane was cheaper to build because of the simplicity of structure, and that a higher speed was attainable through less head resistance. Nieuport also felt that the Bleriot design could be cleaned up, and proceeded to build the most streamlined planes of their time. Competition between Bleriot and Nieuport ran high as they moved into the third International Air Races, held at Eastchurch, England, during a 1-day race meet Saturday, July 1. There was exhibition flying and the Gordon Bennett Cup Race, the feature event.

An unexpected crowd of over 10,000 people made for out-of-the-way Eastchurch to see the events, going mostly by train, although 200 motorcars brought up to a thousand, and some journeyed by air.

The day prior to the race several of the pilots tried out their machines, and again early Saturday, the day of the race, Nieuport of France, Hamel and Ogilvie of England, and Weymann of the United States were all making tests. Weymann's 100-hp Gnome rotary engined Nieuport was timed faster than Hamel's Bleriot, which was powered by an identical engine; this showing prompted M. Louis Bleriot to clip the wing ends of Hamel's machine down to 17-ft. span in an effort to increase its speed.

At 2:50 P.M. Hamel of England was flagged off to be the first entrant in the Bennett race, which was 25 laps over a course about 3.75 miles around, for a total distance of nearly 94 miles. After passing the first mark tower (a scattering pylon placed outside the course to space the racers) too sharply, Hamel, in trying to get around to the racecourse before building up sufficient flying speed, was unable to recover from his steep bank. To the alarm of the onlookers, he came crashing to earth with such terrific force that the rotary engine, still revolving wide open, bounded along for some 60 feet, carrying and breaking up the machine on its way. By sheer luck, Hamel was thrown clear of the tangled wreckage. Beyond a severe shaking and bruising, he was none the worse for his smash!

Then at 3 P.M. Chevalier, one of the French champions, took off in his Nieuport No. 12. Although his 28-hp motor was cutting out at times, he kept up for 11 full laps and was just completing the 12th at 3:45 when he was forced down a quarter-mile from the finish line, breaking his undercarriage and wheels.

Barely three minutes before Chevalier went out of the running, America's Weymann, in his Nieuport, flew over the starting line. The increase in speed was instantly noticeable. By the time he had finished the race at about 4:56 P.M., it was believed that the winner was already found, for Weymann had flown over the course in 1 hr. 11 min. 36.2 sec., for an average speed of 78 mph.

In the meantime, Chevalier took off at 4:40 P.M. in another machine, but fared even worse than on his first mount, for within a few minutes he was forced down with engine trouble—in the same field and within 500 yards of the same spot where he landed with his first machine. He was thus completely out of the running. (They were now permitted two chances to complete the course.)

Just before 4:30, Alec Ogilvie of England brought out his Baby Wright powered with an N.E.C. water-cooled 50-hp engine, and was soon up to the starting line and away. The new note in the music of the two Wright propellers, and the fact that the machine was the only biplane in the race, created fresh interest amongst the crowd. But the "Baby" was soon passed by the cleaner monoplanes, first by Weymann's Nieuport and later by Leblanc's 100-hp Gnome-engined Bleriot and M. Nieuport's 70-hp Gnome-engined plane. (Leblanc on his start cautiously took a wide sweep around the mark towers, for, as on Hamel's machine, Louis Bleriot had cut down the span of Leblanc's monoplane, sacrificing some stability, control, and lift for more speed.)

As had been foreseen, no one bettered Weymann's speed, and the heartiest congratulations were accorded the American champion by both the French and the British competitors, amid cheers from the public. Finishing behind Weymann's winning 78 mph were Leblanc, Nieuport, and then Ogilvie with speeds of 75.8 mph, 75.1 mph, and 53.3 mph respectively.

At this meet, M. Nieuport's clean design and careful attention to small details had proven his planes' superiority over other craft of equal horsepower. Future aircraft design was to be greatly influenced by Nieuport's contribution to the science, and speeds of 100 mph were in the offing.

The Baby Wright Racer which Brookins was to fly in the Bennett Cup Race, shown here in early October 1910 at Simms Station near Dayton, Ohio, where it was constructed and test-flown prior to shipment by train to Belmont, N.Y., for the race. (U.S. Air Force Museum)

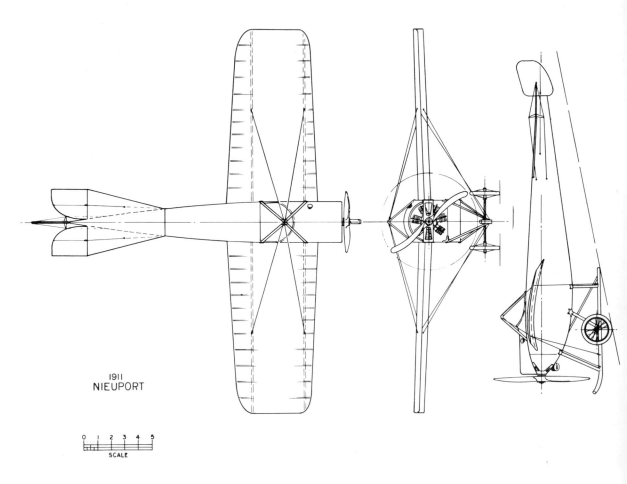

1911
NIEUPORT

0 1 2 3 4 5
SCALE

D.W. CARTER 11/18/66

The Nieuport type monoplane that Charles Weymann flew to victory in the 1911 James Gordon Bennett Cup Race.
(Charles G. Mandrake)

The Baby Wright Racer of 1910, the first of several of its type, was one of the first Wright aircraft to be fitted with wheels. Although its pilot sat erect directly in the slipstream to add drag, the aircraft was quite fast for its 50 hp engine because of its low total frontal area. Photo taken at Simms Station in early October 1910. Pilot unidentified. Handlebar mustache probably acted as a drift indicator!
(U.S. Air Force Museum)

Ah, the sweetness of a propeller blast in one's face, the wonderful smell of burning alcohol and castor oil in the nostrils! What a feeling of achievement the pioneer aeronaut must have experienced flying his untrustworthy steed against the elements! Jules Vedrines of France is seen here about to make his start in the Paris-Madrid Race May 22, 1911, which he won in his Morane. Note whirling 7-cylinder Gnome rotary engine.
(U.S. Air Force)

1912 – James Gordon Bennett Cup Race

The rapid progress in practical applications of aerodynamics has been unparalleled in the history of science. In late 1911 a young French engineer, M. Bechereau, designed for the newly formed French firm of Deperdussin a monoplane that suddenly brought the speed of aircraft above that of the automobile and locomotive. Only above the speed of these earthbound forms of transportation could the airplane be truly useful.

M. Bechereau, only one year graduated from a Paris engineering school, had studied the Bleriot and Nieuport designs, and then improved on these by building a cigar-shaped fuselage, round like the Gnome rotary engine it wore, and cowling the engine to conform to the fuselage lines. By covering the spoke wheels with discs and streamlining the landing-gear legs to a minimum, he made his craft the cleanest of its day. Indeed, it was far ahead of its time, for many designers thought it too radical, mainly because of its landing speed of more than 60 mph. On Feb. 22, 1912, at Pau, France, pilot Jules Vedrines flew a Deperdussin over a straightaway course at the then amazing speed of 100.2 mph.

The Deperdussin firm built several fast ships, and then set about planning for the Gordon Bennett Cup, for only the fastest three ships could represent France. As was expected, Deperdussins piloted by Vedrines and Prevost were first and second in the competition, while Andre Frey was third in a Hanriot monoplane, copied from the Nieuport.

The French speed trio arrived in the United States with the world's three fastest aircraft, only to learn that they were to fly without competition. The English pilots, Claude Grahame-White and Hamel, were unable to come across the Atlantic, and the Burgess Company of the United States was unable to get their slower Nieuport-copied monoplane ready in time.

Glenn Curtiss and the Wright Company were still doggedly building biplanes and were busily filling orders for them, and so they did not build any race planes.

Vedrines' special Deperdussin was an exceptionally streamlined and neat craft for its day and had wheel and rudder foot bar controls — conventional, as we know them today. Ailerons, however, were still missing; the wing-tip trailing edges acted as ailerons and were warped up and down by turning

The 1912 Bennett winning Deperdussin was not as refined in finish as the 1913 models. Note crude seam weld in engine cowl that was not cleaned up for the race.
(National Archives)

The first Deperdussin built was powered by a Gnome rotary engine of only 50 hp. It became, after several tries by Jules Vedrines, the first aircraft to exceed 100 mph—speed 100.22 mph at Pau, France, February 22, 1912. First Deperdussins were easily identified as they carried only two struts on each of their two cabanes. (Musée de l'Air)

This Hanriot monoplane, flown in the 1912 Bennett by Andre Frey, was almost an exact copy of the 1911 Bennett-winning Nieuport. With this type landing gear the pilot had to make a four-point landing—two wheels and back end of skids, no tail skid being employed. Skids were turned up at the front like skis and extended well forward to prevent nose overs. (Musée de l'Air)

Built later in 1912 this Bennett-winning Deperdussin was powered by a 160 hp Gnome rotary engine. Note small rise head-rest, two three-strut cabane braces, and still no windshield! Mechanic has just primed engine with raw petrol and Vedrines awaits crank for test hop at the factory. (Musée de l'Air)

Vedrines' Deperdussin overtaking Frey's Hanriot. He went on to win the 1912-Bennett race with an average speed of 105.5 mph.

the wheel control. The controls were the especial delight of Vedrines, for he said that he could maintain his flyer in perfect poise with the thumb and forefinger of his left hand.

The fuselage was built up of wood-lattice girders, covered with 3-ply wood veneer. The wing panels were built up of hickory spars, I-ribs of pine and ash, the leading edges plywood covered, and the whole wing covered with fabric treated with several coats of varnish. The wings were braced by stranded-steel cable.

Race day, September 9, was cloudless and hot but relieved by a fair breeze across the ground at Clearing in the neighborhood of Chicago, scene for the contest.

Vedrines made his start at 10:00 A.M. in his beautiful little Deperdussin, soon to be followed by Andre Frey in his Hanriot, and then Prevost, who flew a Deperdussin similar to that of Vedrines. Vedrines' plane was powered by a 160-hp 14-cyl. (twin rows of 7 cylinders each) Gnome rotary engine. The other two planes wore the same type of engine but were of only 100 horsepower.

Bumpy air kept the pilots busy as the planes tossed and rocked, often requiring a liberal margin in rounding the pylons. The turns, though 60° at each pylon, were made with suddenness. The planes would shoot like an arrow straight for the turning point, bank suddenly round the pylon, recover instantly, and then scoot on down the course only a few yards above the earth. When a lumbering biplane plodded over the racecourse, it seemed to stand still as the racers shot beneath.

Vedrines, with his engine running perfectly, finished the 30-lap 124.8-mile course in 1 hr. 10 min. and 56 sec., his speed averaging 105.5 mph.

Frey dropped out with engine trouble on the 24th lap, after averaging 94.3 mph. Prevost, of whom we will read more later, flying steadily, finished the racecourse with an average of 103.8 mph.

And so Vedrines of France was adjudged the winner with Prevost second. During his race for the Cup, Vedrines beat the world's speed record for 20 km (12.4 miles), covering the distance in 6 min. 56 sec. at a speed of 107 mph.

◆   ◆   ◆

1913 – Schneider Trophy Race

Glenn Curtiss, after many trials, had in June, 1910, made the world's first take-off and alighting on water near his factory at Hammondsport, N. Y. His designs gave this nation the lead in seaplane development for many years, but France, which was leading the world in aviation, was quick to see the hydro-aeroplane's many advantages and jumped quickly into this new phase. However, by late 1912, Jacques Schneider, a wealthy French aviation enthusiast, felt that water aircraft were not being developed as speedily as they could be, and so he presented a trophy, the award designating an annual race over open water by seaworthy seaplanes. The nation winning the race three times in succession was to be permanent owner of the trophy, which was valued at £1,000. There was another £1,000 in cash prizes offered each year for the first three years.

Destined to become the world's most famous all-time air races, the first International hydro-aeroplane race for the Schneider Trophy was held during a water meet at Monaco, on the French Riviera, in April, 1913.

Qualifying tests began on April 3. Three French pilots and one American passed the tests. The French pilots were: Prevost flying a Deperdussin, Garros in a Morane-Saulnier, and Espanet in a Nieuport. The American pilot, Weymann, also flew a Nieuport. All four seaplanes were twin-float monoplanes, and were powered with Gnome 14-cyl. twin-row rotary engines that delivered 160 hp at 1,200 rpm. The Deperdussin was the least streamlined of the four aircraft, be-cause the alighting gear was a maze of bracing struts and wires. Certainly M. Bechereau, the Deperdussin designer, had not developed this gear!

The Schneider Trophy Race was held on Tuesday morning, April 6, over a 28-lap course for a total distance of 174 miles (280 km).

Prevost was the first away at 8:05, followed at 8:19 by Garros. Espanet started at 8:50, and Weymann at 9:14. Garros did not go very far, dropping out with engine trouble. Then Espanet was forced down, after his first lap, because of a fuel-line failure. The race therefore resolved itself into a duel between Prevost and Weymann. Weymann took the lead in the fourth lap, but after completing it — 200 km (124.27 miles) mark — he too encountered engine trouble and set his little Nieuport down safely. He had averaged 68.8 mph. This left Prevost to win as he liked. He skimmed low past the finish line and alighted. Then, however, at the request of the judges, he reflew part of the last lap, with the timers' watches still running, as there was some doubt as to whether he had turned outside one course marker.

Prevost had averaged only 45.8 mph to win the first Schneider Trophy Race, but his speed would have been closer to 60 mph had he not been timed during his refly of the last marker.

France now led the world in both sea- and land-plane types, and her experience provided designers with priceless data for building seaplanes with which to patrol her shores during the forthcoming war.

◆ ◆ ◆

Closeup of Charles Weymann's Nieuport as Weymann, right, and his mechanic await their turn in the Schneider Race. He flew a higher average speed than the winner before dropping out with engine trouble. (*Musée de l'Air*)

*Weymann taking the lead in the fourth lap. He dropped out later with engine
trouble, and Prevost (top) won the 1913 Schneider race with an average speed
of 45.75 mph.*

This beautifully clean Deperdussin seaplane was especially built and groomed for Prevost to fly in the 1913 Schneider Race but engine trouble prevented qualification. Setting is Monaco Harbor.   *(Musée de l'Air)*

After French pilot Prevost learned that his special Deperdussin would be unable to fly, his race number 19 was quickly painted on this earlier vintage Deperdussin which the French team had been using to acquaint themselves with the race course. Prevost flew it to victory, braces, struts, wires and all!   *(Musée de l'Air)*

Mechanic obligingly holds tail up for a good shot of the Nieuport (Race No. 3) flown by French pilot Espanet in the Schneider. Craft dropped out in 1st lap with a broken fuel line.
(Musée de l'Air)

Espanet in his Nieuport (Race No. 3) at bottom of ramp used to enter and leave water. Aircraft has just been towed to ramp by a rowboat after fuel line broke in the race.
(Musée de l'Air)

Morane-Saulnier (Race No. 1) piloted by Raymond Garros is seen dropping out of a Schneider in the first lap due to engine trouble. Small sailboat with two judges is moored to one of the race course marker buoys.
(Musée de l'Air)

Weymann (Race No. 6 on rudder) flies near a Nieuport (Race No. 5) that is just taking off. The Nieuport, pilot unknown, did not qualify but was not needed as France entered the race with their allowable three that did qualify.
(Musée de l'Air)

1913 – James Gordon Bennett Cup Race

Once again the International Air Races were held at Rheims, France, scene of the first important races.

The meeting opened on Saturday morning, September 27, with the French elimination trials to determine their three fastest entries for the Bennett Cup race. There were two afternoon events — one for height and the other for slow speed.

The altitude contest was held on each of the three days of the race meet. Gilbert of France led in all three sections for the three days, with 19,033 feet for pilot only, 14,265 feet with one passenger, and 11,936 feet with two passengers.

Sunday's program, September 28, included a speed test, the daily altitude contest, and a cross-country race. Then on Monday, September 29, came the high-speed event, the by now world-famous James Gordon Bennett Cup Race.

England, the United States, and Germany had withdrawn from the Bennett contest, probably because they could not equal the wonderful performance of France's aircraft. The only other country represented was Belgium, and her pilot, Crombez, flew a French Deperdussin. Prevost, Gilbert, and Vedrines flew for France, the first two pilots using Deperdussins and Vedrines a Ponnier, which followed the lines of its predecessor the Hanriot, which in turn had been copied from the Nieuport. All four entries were powered with identical 14-cyl. 160-hp Gnome rotary twin-row engines.

The Deperdussins designed by M. Bechereau for this race were the ultimate in streamlining for their day. A big propeller nose spinner graced the nose, and a tight-fitting cowl faired the engine into the fuselage. The landing gear was faired more cleanly into the fuselage, and so clean was the general design that it can be seen duplicated in the Travel-Air "Mystery" racer of 1929. Indeed, with equal horsepower, the Deperdussin of 1913 would outperform the U.S. Army Ryan PT-22 trainer of World War II!

The Bennett race was still flown against time, the pilots taking their planes off one by one, but individual piloting ability was, of course, a main factor.

Crombez was first away at 10 A.M. on Monday morning, but it was soon seen that, barring accidents, the Cup was not likely to leave France, for Crombez played his pylon turns very safe. Flying very regularly, he completed the full course of 20 laps with a time 1 minute and 3 seconds better than that of Jules Vedrines' in his winning flight at Chicago in 1912. But, as it turned out, Crombez' time was the slowest of the day, giving him fourth place in the race.

Prevost, who had earlier in the year won the Schneider Trophy Race, was next to go. At 11:15 he started off in his Deperdussin at "an alarming pace" and soon showed that the smaller wings installed just before the race (less than 20 feet) had materially assisted his speed. Flying very low, about 60 feet above the ground, and rising 15 feet or so at each pylon, Prevost banked steeply and dived around the corners nearly clipping the pylons, just as Curtiss had flown in winning the 1909 Bennett. This type of pylon turn was used for years until "groove" pilots flying at

Crombez of Belgium, race No. 17, about to be released by ground crew for his start in the Bennett. Crombez flew an early 1912 model Deperdussin in the race, did not take pylons closely, so finished 4th and last. (Musée de l'Air)

This excellent view shows Prevost making pylon turn in Bennett. Photo shows aircraft to be no more than 25 feet above ground. *(Warren M. Bodie)*

Emile Vedrines, seen banking around one of the course markers in his clean little Ponnier, flew the straightaways a bit high, dived as he turned pylons. Some early race pilots thought this method superior to steady altitude groove flying. *(Musée de l'Air)*

Emile Vedrines all fired up and ready for takeoff in the Bennett Race. Note absence of ailerons, wing warping being used, as on Deperdussin aircraft. *(Musée de l'Air)*

Here is the Deperdussin brought to its sleekest refinement, complete with headrest and wind-shield. Gilbert, Race No. F2, seen here taking off for the Bennett Race, had a sour engine throughout the course, finished 3rd. *(Musée de l'Air)*

Prevost flew entry F1 with no windshield as he felt it would slow his Deperdussin, wore a seat belt and shoulder harness. Prevost's ship is easily identified as it was fitted with the tallest headrest ever seen on any Deperdussin. This interesting photo was taken by a daring photographer from atop one of the pylons as Prevost began turn. Top of wheel control can be seen in cockpit just ahead of pilot.   (U.S. Air Force)

Emile Vedrines has just warmed up his engine, shut it off, and now awaits his turn to take-off in the Bennett. What looks like a small opaque wind screen in front of Emile is in reality some person's hat. The silver Ponnier F-5 was an almost exact copy of the 1912 Hanriot racer which was, in turn, an almost identical ship to the 1911 racing Nieuport.

(Musée de l'Air)

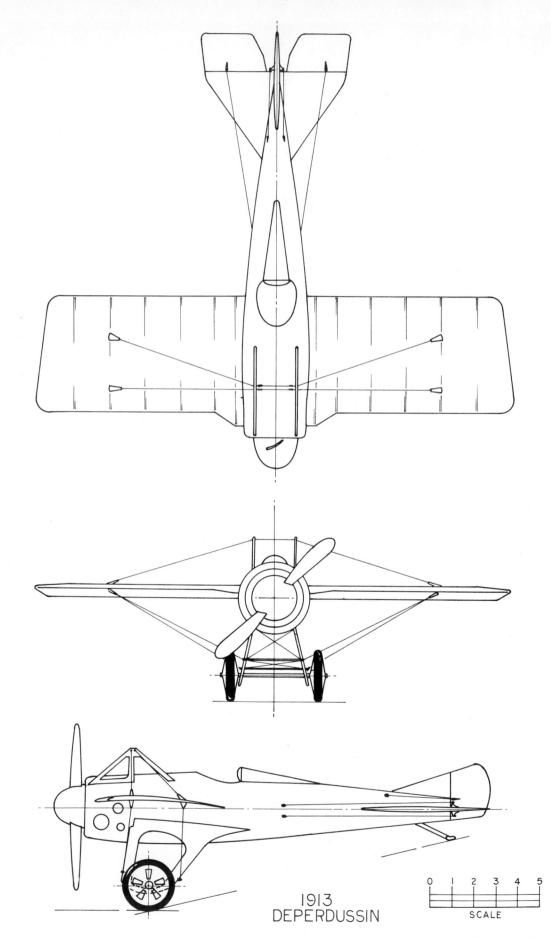

1913
DEPERDUSSIN

0 1 2 3 4 5
SCALE

D.W. CARTER 3/25/66

Monocoque fuselage of the Deperdussin was built up of 1/8" three-ply tulip wood covered on both sides with linen fabric which was glued on and then varnished several coats. Wing spars were of hickory and ash wood with pine ribs, and covering was doped linen. All Deperdussin aircraft were described as being chocolate in color. *(Musée de l'Air)*

Fixed tail surfaces of all Deperdussins were built up of plywood covered on the outside with linen glued on, then varnished. Movable tail surfaces were built up of wood, then fabric covered. Bechereau obtained ultra-sleek finish on all his Deperdussin aircraft by using several coats of varnish and sandpapering the finish between each coat, like cabinet work.
(Musée de l'Air)

steady altitudes disproved the theory. The first round was completed at 127 mph; this and the sixth lap, which was covered in the same time, were the fastest in the race. Prevost covered the 124.3-mile course in 59 min. 45.6 sec., his average speed being 124.5 mph.

Gilbert started third in his Deperdussin, but his first lap took over three minutes and showed that his machine was a good deal slower than Prevost's. It took him 1 hr. 2 min. 55 sec., to cover the course for an average of 119.5 mph, which won third place in the race.

Emile Vedrines, no relation to Jules Vedrines, the fourth and last to start, "went off at a great pace" in a Ponnier monoplane. His speed during the first round was 125.5 mph. This proved to be his fastest lap, however. His average speed worked out to 123 mph to secure second place. Vedrines' little Ponnier racer was nearly as clean in design as the Deperdussins, and it seemed that the Ponnier was just as fast on the straightaway as the others, but Vedrines' pylon turns were very wide, losing possible first place, as his total time was but three seconds per lap slower than Prevost's.

Prevost won the race, and France had won the

Bennett for two years straight, almost without competition, with the fastest aircraft in the world. Winning the Schneider as well as the Bennett Trophy was to make 1913 France's best year in racing competition.

Once again the monoplane had proved itself superior, for with equal horsepower, no biplane could come close to it. However, the monoplane was falling into disfavor, for statistics showed that many more deaths were occurring in monoplanes. This was only logical — the monoplanes were faster, they were in greater quantity because of their speed and simplicity features, but they hit the earth from the then unexplainable stalls and spins with greater force. The biplanes, by their very mass, crumbled more on impact and so spared their pilots more often. England banned the monoplane from her military program entirely, and France soon followed. The clean features of the Deperdussin were, as far as possible, worked into the generally stronger-braced biplanes, and so it was that the Allies went into World War I almost entirely on biplanes. But no biplane of that war ever outsped a Deperdussin with near equal power, and few with twice the horsepower exceeded the Deperdussin.

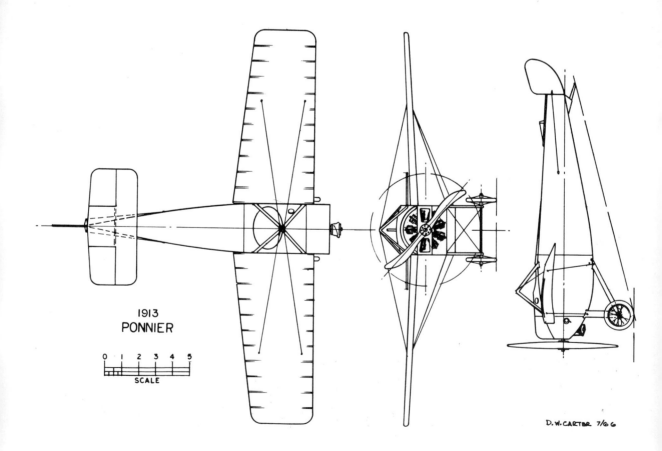

1913
PONNIER

0 1 2 3 4 5
SCALE

D. W. CARTER 7/66

1914 – Schneider Trophy Race

Although France now led the world in aviation, England was coming up fast, for she realized that her island was no longer isolated because of the English Channel. She was building Deperdussins and other French makes under license and buying French engines when her own did not fill the need. Also, England was building many planes of her own design, with Bristol, Roe, and Sopwith supplying many military models.

The United States was still lagging, while Germany was building up for the coming war, for she too realized that progress in military aviation was becoming a must. But neither Germany nor the United States was building the racing aircraft so necessary in the development of military planes.

So once again French entries led in numbers for the 1914 Schneider race, Monday, April 20, again held at Monaco on the French Riviera as France had won the previous Schneider. Competitors present were: Espanet and Pierre Levasseur, Nieuport monoplanes, and Garros, Morane monoplane, for France; C. H. Pixton, Sopwith Tabloid biplane, and Lord Carbery, Deperdussin monoplane, for Great Britain; Burri, F.B.A. biplane, for Switzerland; and Weymann, Nieuport monoplane, and Thaw, Deperdussin monoplane, for the United States. Stoeffler, Germany's entry, had a smash on the previous day, as did Lord Carbery in his Morane, but he borrowed a Deperdussin for the race. All entries were powered by French Gnome rotary air-cooled engines; the Sopwith and F.B.A. with 9-cyl. 100-hp Gnomes, and the others by 14-cyl. 160-hp twin-row Gnomes.

The rules specified that the individual starts must be made between 8 A.M. and sunset. When two bombs were fired at 8 A.M. on Monday, Levasseur, the Frenchman, took off from the calm waters of Monaco Bay into a strong easterly wind. His Nieuport monoplane took a 200-yard run. Next away was Espanet in a similar machine. He made a lightning take-off before the starter had given him the signal. Burri, the Swiss pilot, in his F.B.A. flying boat, the only boat in the races (all others were twin-float seaplanes), was next away. This seaplane had an inherent tendency to porpoise, and its take-off was a series of hops before the machine was airborne.

Pixton, in his Sopwith Tabloid, which had been converted into a single-seat racer, started about 15 minutes later and was into the air after a run of only 60 feet.

Rules of the contest decreed that the competitors be required to taxi across the line before taking off,

then make two descents to the sea at specified points. Then they were to continue the flight proper, the starting line having been crossed in full flight. Total distance was 174 miles, or 280 km.

Pixton executed the rules superbly, but the other pilots had difficulty. Burri had to cope with a machine which bounced like a football every time it contacted the water, and his efforts caused great excitement.

Pixton's first lap lost him only 17 seconds, and as he roared around the course he turned the markers acutely in 70° banks.

The Continental spectators, accustomed to their own machines winning race after race, had never seen such flying and were loud in their praise.

For an hour or so the Sopwith kept buzzing round lap after lap with impressive regularity. During the 15th lap, the Gnome of the Sopwith began to misfire. Pixton kept going for the rest of the race, although the engine was running on only eight of its nine cylinders. Finally, at the end of the 28th (and last) lap, Pixton crossed the finishing line accompanied by the roar of an enthusiastic crowd. His time was 2 hrs. 13.4 sec., with an average speed of 86.8 mph.

Pixton then opened up his engine and tore around for another two laps at still higher speed. The little Sopwith responded magnificently and broke the world's record for seaplanes, with a speed of 92 mph for a total distance of 300 km.

Meanwhile, other competitors were crawling around. Lord Carbery, the other British pilot, flying a Deperdussin monoplane, got off all right, but after alighting in the first lap, could not get off again because of engine trouble. Espanet had to alight after 17 laps, and Levasseur had a similar fate after 18 laps. The rear banks of their twin-row rotary motors were overheating, a common source of trouble. Burri, in the bounding F.B.A. flying boat, completed 20 laps and then alighted to refuel. He had some trouble in taking off with full tanks, but eventually got off and finished the race, to win second place.

The rest of the competitors were dismayed by the Sopwith's performance and did not start, for only the winner received a prize.

The Sopwith was the most streamlined entry this year and justly deserved to win, for although a biplane, it was the smallest aircraft in the race; its wings were thin and its alighting gear was cleanest by far.

Repeated troubles with the twin-row engines influenced aircraft design throughout the coming war,

The winning Sopwith Tabloid passing the F.B.A. flying boat. Espanet's Nieuport (No. 6) was forced down with engine trouble. C. H. Pixton piloted the 1914 Schneider winning plane at an average speed of 87.75 mph.

for all rotary engines used in the conflict were single-row. Later, when more power was needed, water-cooled engines were developed.

Later this year events transpired which were to affect, directly and indirectly, the whole course of Allied aviation throughout the war. Armand Deperdussin, as farsighted as he was dishonest, went to jail on stock swindling charges. Louis Bleriot, in order to preserve the engineering talent of the Deperdussin firm and that of Bechereau in particular, took over the grounds and sheds near Paris and formed the now famous *Societé Pour Aviation et Derives* (S.P.A.D.). After war was declared, Papa Bleriot guided Bechereau in his wartime Spad designs, aircraft whose history will live forever.

◆   ◆   ◆

C. Howard Pixton's Schneider winning aircraft was practically a stock Sopwith Tabloid Scout, several of which were built, beginning in 1913. Twin main floats and a ventral tail float with a small rudder was fitted and the fuel capacity was increased by 30 gallons by fitting an extra tank beside the pilot's seat. The 100 hp Gnome Monosoupape nine-cylinder rotary engine had just appeared, so one was fitted to the Tabloid. *(Musée de l'Air)*

Pilot Burri being towed to a beaching ramp after finishing 2nd in the Schneider. His Franco-British Seaplane (F.B.A.) was the only seaplane in the race, also wore the new Monosoupape 100 hp engine which was lighter in weight to horsepower than previous rotary engines. *(Musée de l'Air)*

1920 – Schneider Trophy Race

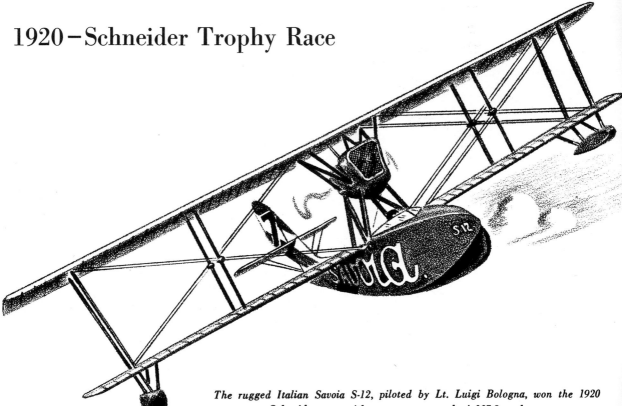

*The rugged Italian Savoia S-12, piloted by Lt. Luigi Bologna, won the 1920
Schneider race with an average speed of 107.2 mph.*

During World War I, Italy developed many fine military flying boats, and she appeared in Bournemouth, England, scene of the first postwar Schneider race, with the fastest entry. The race, on April 20, 1919, was flown in a dense fog, and the British and French contestants soon dropped out, unable to find their way around the water course. Italian pilot Janello, in his Savoia S-13 biplane flying boat, was the only pilot to finish the course, but unfortunately for him, he regularly flew around a buoy which he believed to be a course marker. The race was declared NO CONTEST. As reward for her effort, Italy was intrusted with the organization of the 1920 contest.

In 1920, only the Italian team survived the trials. The only pilot to undertake the navigability tests in the rough sea and winds of September 18 was Navy Lt. Luigi Bologna, flying a 500-hp Ansaldo-engined Savoia S-12 flying boat ruggedly built for bad-weather flying. He completed the tests and on the following day, the scheduled day for the races, attempted to fly over the triangular course that lay just outside Venice Lagoon. He gave up after 5 laps because of the squally winds. Bologna tried again on September 22, and covered the full course, 10 laps around the 22.2-mile course, averaging 107.2 mph, and was declared the winner of the race.

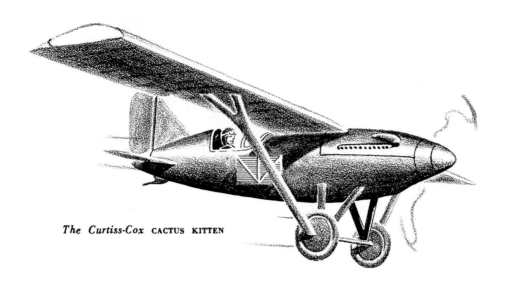

The Curtiss-Cox CACTUS KITTEN

1920 – James Gordon Bennett Cup Race

The nation holding the world's speed record has invariably led the world in aviation, and so it was that France led the Allies to air supremacy during World War I, supplying not always the fastest but by far the most fighting planes. England contributed heavily too, but the United States rallied only in time to furnish training planes for her own pilots and, near the war's end, a relatively few English SE-5 fighters and two-place DeHavilland bomber-observation planes built under license.

Settling down from the effects of war, France was anxious to get on with the Gordon Bennett Cup Race, for she had made a poor showing in the 1920 Schneider race trials and had only to win the Bennett Cup once more to gain permanent possession. England and the United States took up the challenge, for they realized fully by now the importance of air power, and that today's racing craft became the pursuit plane of tomorrow.

The United States sent four aircraft abroad in quest of the Cup. Three of them were newly built pure racing craft, the only ones to appear, for all the rest were reworked pursuit types.

The Curtiss Company built two racers on order for Texas oilman S. E. J. Cox, and both were shipped to France for the race. The fuselages of both planes were identical, plywood in construction, powered with Curtiss V-12 435-hp engines, with rectangular water radiators along each side of the fuselage and the cockpits fully enclosed for the first time in history. One ship, the *Cactus Kitten*, was a thick-winged monoplane, and the other ship, the *Texas Wildcat*, was a biplane with double-cambered wings, the first ever used. Both were built without regard to landing speed, for the airfields of France were supposedly spacious. Such was not the case, however, and the faster landing *Cactus Kitten* was not assembled for the race. A hurried take-off without checking the airdrome at Morane-Saulnier Field just outside Paris, where the landing gear was weakened by an obstruction in the tall grass, caused the *Texas Wildcat* to roll into splinters upon landing at Etampes, scene of the races. Curtiss test pilot Roland Rohlfs escaped with only a dislocated shoulder, several cuts about the head, and a very black eye.

The U. S. Air Service entry and their first racing plane was a Verville Scout biplane VCP-1, with the usual Hispano-Suiza engine replaced by a new 12-cyl. V-type Packard engine rated at 638 hp at 2,000 rpm. The cooling radiator was of the honeycomb type, rectangular, and was placed under the lower wing's leading edge. The Verville was built entirely of wood and plywood, and the tapered wings and movable surfaces were fabric covered. This plane was by far the most powerful at the race meet.

The Dayton-Wright Airplane Company, with Orville Wright as consulting engineer, built and sent to France by far the most interesting plane of the races. This little craft was one of the first to have a retractable landing gear — a type the Grumman Aircraft Company many years later incorporated into their famous Navy biplane fighters and their later Wildcat monoplane fighter. The little plane's full-cantilever wing was built of solid balsa with chunks cut out, and the wing then covered with plywood. The wing leading and trailing edges were hinged so that the pilot could adjust the wing camber at will, an innovation that many years later gave aircraft wing flaps for faster take-offs and slower landings. The pilot was completely enclosed inside the cabin and could see only through windows at the side. For landing, the pilot could push the side windows open with

The Dayton-Wright drops out of the race as Sadi-Lecointe (No. 10), in his Nieuport,
flies on to win the 1920 Bennett with an average speed of 168.5 mph, followed by
de Romanet, who finished in second place.

The Dayton-Wright Racer, designed by Milton C. Baumann, was officially designated the RB Racer. View shows actuating rods for increasing wing camber on take-off and landing. Note leading and trailing edges depressed; mechanism was operated by hand crank on instrument panel which also actuated retractable landing gear. Original camber-change device, seen here, had two actuating arms on each side of wing top. *(U.S. Air Force Museum)*

Reports were various as to reason Dayton-Wright Racer dropped out of the race. One account stated the left rudder cable broke (doubtful), another that some scoundrel applied an acid to the left rudder cable which ate away the cable in flight (possible). A third account stated that its pilot, Howard Rinehart, was unable to crank the wing to its high-speed or flat contour and, of course, fully retract its landing gear which cranked up and down with wing camber change (probable). *(U.S. Air Force Museum)*

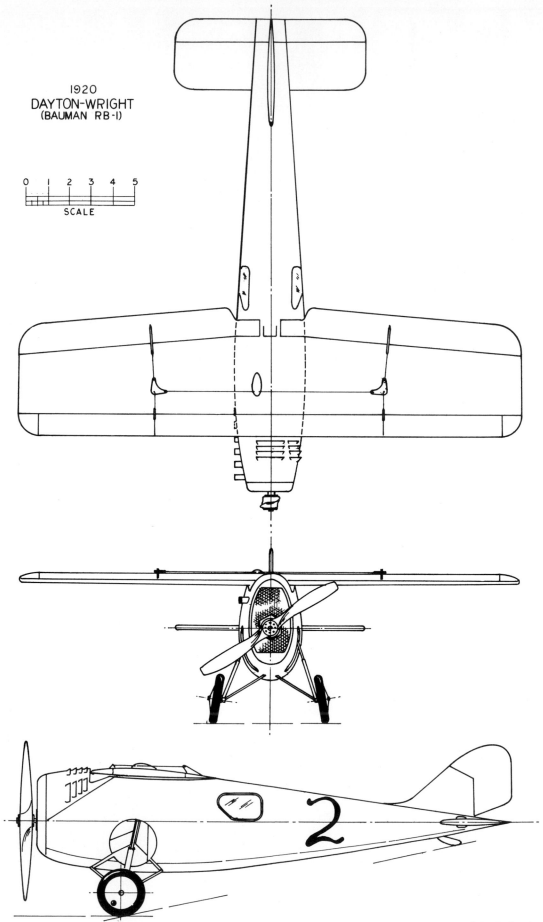

1920
DAYTON-WRIGHT
(BAUMAN RB-1)

0 1 2 3 4 5
SCALE

2

D.W. CARTER 10/66

This view also shows Dayton-Wright with two actuating rods on each side of wing top, its original configuration. Entire aircraft was covered with plywood, including movable control surfaces. Linen was then glued over the plywood, then varnished several coats, much like the pre-WWI Deperdussin aircraft. (U.S. Air Force Museum)

The Dayton-Wright did 165 mph on a practice lap of the Bennett course with engine not open, years ahead with features that were all eventually to be used on other aircraft. Reputedly it would do 200 mph with its 250-hp Hall-Scott Special engine. Actual aircraft can be seen today in the Henry Ford Museum at Dearbon, Mich. (Musée de l'Air)

Dayton-Wright Racer as it appeared at the Bennett Race with but one actuating rod on each side of wing top, which could account for possible failure to change camber properly. Pilot entered aircraft through trap door above cockpit, could open side windows by hand or, on landings, open them by leaning shoulder against back of frame and pushing forward, thus keeping hands free. (Musée de l'Air)

Martinsyde Semiquaver, a modified pursuit plane flown by Raynham, was the only English entry. Like all French entries it was powered by a 320 hp Hispano-Suiza V-8 engine.
(Musée de l'Air)

Converted from a war-surplus DH9 as a test bed for a new Napier Lion engine of 450 hp, this DeHavilland DH9R achieved a closed circuit record of 145 mph at First Air Traffic Exhibition in Amsterdam in 1919. This speed was later raised to 149.43 mph.
(Napier)

Borel biplane powered by a 320 hp Hispano engine and piloted by M. Barrault in French elimination trials, where it lost out to other entries. Small vertical fin and rudder must have presented control problems at slow speeds.
(Musée de l'Air)

Top wing was gulled into fuselage on this SPAD HERBEMONT for the race but ship, flown by M. Casale, failed to qualify. Wing and tail surfaces of both SPAD aircraft were built up of wood spars and ribs, fabric covered. Fuselages were of plywood, fabric covered.
(Musée de l'Air)

Curtiss-Cox Cactus Kitten was built with two sets of wings and is seen here with the long wing. Brace strut has initial fabric tape applied to hold balsa wood fairing in place for more complete wrap and fairing. Photo taken at Curtiss factory before final paint job—red fuselage and silver wings and tail—was applied. (Charles G. Mandrake)

This view of the Curtiss-Cox Cactus Kitten shows aircraft with its optional wing, of shorter span but quite a lot thicker in section, with extending ailerons. Note different wing brace strut than that used on the thinner winged Kitten. Wide-bladed wood propeller has extremely high pitch for best take-off at expense of a long take-off run. (Charles G. Mandrake)

This post-WWI SPAD HERBEMONT, flown by Bernard de Romanet in the Bennett, was practically a stock two-seater production line aircraft with the rear cockpit covered for the race. Race No. 8 was painted on fuselage after this photo was taken. (Musée de l'Air)

Sharp photo of a Nieuport Model 29 taken later in 1920, as it appeared for an annual French-held event, the Deutsch de la Meurthe Cup Race. Piloted by M. Lasne, the aircraft won the race. (U.S. Air Force)

Here is the Nieuport Model 29 flown by Kirch, in its original and conventional configuration. Aircraft was stock in that several were built identical to each other on assembly lines as pursuit types. (Musée de l'Air)

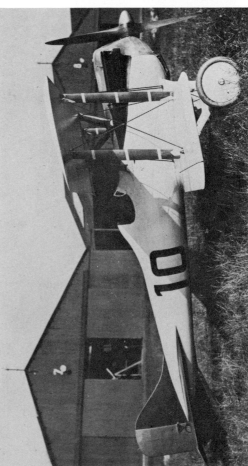

This Nieuport 29 flown to victory by Sadi-Lecointe was a sister ship to No. 11 flown by Kirch and was powered by the 320 hp Hispano V8 water-cooled engines. All Nieuport entries wore Lamblin-type radiators to cool engine water. (Musée de l'Air)

At first glance this Nieuport is a conventional open cockpit biplane. Closer inspection shows cockpit and a tear-drop shaped peephole below cockpit to be flush, covered with transparent material and its pilot, M. Kirch, is seen peering out the side! Musée de l'Air says Kirch flew this configuration in Bennett, which would account for its being faster than the winning ship before dropping out.

(Musée de l'Air)

The Curtiss-Cox Cactus Kitten monoplane and the Texas Wildcat biplane were probably the first aircraft with water-cooled engines that had a fuselage built up of plywood that ran its entire length. Only metal in the fuselage was the motor mount and engine top cowl. Craft were also the first to have transparent cockpit hatches, which had to be installed after pilot was in cockpit. This view shows neat wheel fairing which also acted as a mud scraper.

(Dustin W. Carter)

his head and could then see quite well. Very narrow but extremely deep, the fuselage was plywood. Powered by a 6-cyl. in-line Hall-Scott 250-hp engine with a nose radiator, this little ship was the only monoplane at the races and was by far the cleanest in design.

The English and French entries were all conventional pursuit biplanes, cleaned up for the race and powered with the 320-hp Hispano-Suiza V-type water-cooled engine.

It was a dull, misty morning at the Villesauvage airdrome of Etampes when, at 7 A.M. on September 28, the competitors arrived from their various hotels at Etampes and Paris. The clouds were low and visibility poor, weather that seemed the rule rather than the exception for European air races.

As time wore on, motorcars began to arrive from Paris, and one could see the famous French constructors Henri Farman, Louis Bleriot, Rene Caudron, Delage and Bazaine of Nieuports, Robert Morane, Louis Breguet, and young Marcel Hanriot; and famous pilots such as Weymann, Prevost, and Leblanc. They and other race pilots had been little heard of during World War I, for they saw little combat but were retained as test and consulting pilots.

At a little past 1 P.M. the sun broke through occasionally to improve the weather some, and there was a stirring about the machines at the far end of the airdrome. At 1:25, the Nieuport biplane, piloted by Kirch of France, came racing by the stands, took off, and cruised around for a few minutes. Having got his engine warmed up, Kirch approached the starting line and, with a dip salute of his wings, was off. About 20 minutes later he was followed by Bernard de Romanet of France in a Spad. Sadi-Lecointe of France was next off at 2:10 in his French Nieuport. A few minutes later Howard Rinehart, of the United States, got off in the little Dayton-Wright monoplane, and after circling the airdrome to retract his wheels into the fuselage, crossed the starting line and disappeared down the course. At 2:35 Maj. "Shorty" Schroeder of the U. S. team was off and roared over the line in his Army Verville-Packard.

In the meantime Kirch completed his first lap at 181.5 mph, which later proved to be the fastest lap of the day. Returning after the second lap, Kirch was forced to land because of "sooted-up" spark plugs. De Romanet in the Spad was next to complete his first

lap and was around the marker and away on his second lap, averaging 162 mph.

The Dayton-Wright then flew into view, and, to the surprise of many and the dismay of all Americans, the landing wheels began to emerge. Rinehart made a beautiful landing and reported that he was unable to turn left. Examination showed that the left rudder cable was broken.

Soon afterward the Verville-Packard hove into sight and it too landed; with that America's last hopes were gone. It was later determined that the Verville did not carry enough radiator area to cool the 638-hp Packard engine, and the carburetor air intake was faulty at full throttle causing flames to pour out the exhaust pipes, with the danger of fire ever present.

On completion of his second lap, de Romanet landed, but after adjustments took off again, although by then the delay seemed too much. His total time for the 186.4 miles was 1 hr. 39 min. 6.6 sec., for an average speed of but 113.5 mph. During his last lap, an oil leak smothered him with oil. He had to raise his goggles and was blinded by the oil but somehow managed to make a safe landing. Certainly none begrudged plucky little de Romanet his second place.

Meanwhile Sadi-Lecointe of France was methodically flying the course, with beautiful turns at the pylons. He landed after completing the full course in 1 hr. 6 min. 17.2 sec. to average 168.5 mph.

It was not until about 4:30 that Raynham of England had his Martinsyde *Semiquaver* up to the starting line, wisely awaiting the cooler evening air, for he too had radiator-cooling trouble. He completed but one lap and landed with a broken oil pump, and England's only chance was gone.

And so Sadi-Lacointe had won the Gordon Bennett Cup for France's third consecutive win, to gain permanent possession of the Cup and thus end the first chapter in a glorious history of air racing.

This year's Bennett race again proved that the fastest plane alone does not win a race, but that a combination of mechanical perfection and piloting ability is necessary to victory. Sadi-Lacointe had flown his Nieuport over the course time after time until he knew every inch of it, and he and his mechanics had the Nieuport in top order.

Dayton-Wright racer showing landing gear extended.

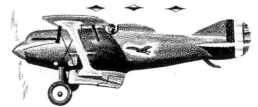

The U.S. Army's first purely racing craft, the Verville-Packard.

1920 — Pulitzer Trophy Race

Since the dawn of history those people who possessed the best and fastest transportation — from horse to aircraft — have led the world. The United States was by now fully aware of this fact and was determined to improve her status, especially after her poor showing in the International Bennett races. Accordingly, newspaperman Ralph Pulitzer, after conferring with receptive U. S. Army and Navy officials, offered a trophy to promote high speed. Plaques and cash prizes were offered, and the race was to be an unlimited free-for-all, restricted only to landing speed, which could not, for safety's sake, exceed 75 mph. All nations were invited.

The first Pulitzer Trophy Race was held at Mitchel Field, Long Island, on Thanksgiving Day, November 27. The course was triangular, from Mitchel Field to Lufberry Field, then to Henry Damm Field, thence back to Mitchel. Entries were to fly four times around a 29.02-mile course for a total of 116.08 miles. The planes were sent off one after another, and each one timed separately.

More aircraft flew in this closed-course race than will ever bend throttles together again, for 37 started and 25 finished. Most of the aircraft were war-surplus or pursuits of postwar design. Of the 12 contestants who did not complete the race, one was disqualified for cutting inside a pylon, while 11 experienced power-plant troubles.

The race was witnessed by at least 25,000 people. The roads following the course were lined with parked cars, and large crowds gathered at the turning points.

Flying the fastest plane of the day with great skill, Army Capt. Corliss Mosely carefully threaded his way through the maze of racers to win the Pulitzer Trophy at a speed of 156.5 mph; then later flew the same machine over a measured mile at 186 mph. The 638-hp Verville-Packard which Mosely flew was the same machine entered in the Gordon Bennett race, with various small changes to improve its speed and reliability.

The Verville-Packard excited great interest, for its wing loading of 14.12 lbs. per sq. ft. was considered enormous, and it was doubtful if constructors, engineers, and military pilots would be converted to the use of such "very high powered" single-seaters. The practical limit for pursuits had previously been considered as being 300 hp.

Second place went to Harold Hartney, who flew a beautiful "groove" race in a Thomas-Morse MB-3 pursuit powered by a 300-hp Wright-Hispano engine. Hartney averaged 148 mph for the course. His plane was a standard military pursuit with only half the engine power of the winner. Manufactured in quantities for the Army Air Service, the MB-3 was all wood with fabric covering and was fairly clean in design. The engine was cooled by fuselage side radiators. In a later flight over a measured mile, Hartney, the famous American ace, succeeded in flying this machine at 177.3 mph.

Third place went to smooth-flying civilian pilot Bert Acosta, who averaged 134.5 mph in an Italian S. V. Ansaldo I Balilla, fitted with an SPA 220-hp engine. This single seater, one of the few entered by a private firm, was a single strutter of very clean design. It was powered by a 6-cyl. vertical in-line engine, cooled by a nose radiator, and the fuselage was deep and narrow with flat sides. Interplane struts were steel, and the plane was of conventional wood and fabric construction.

Lt. St. Clair Streett, commander of the famous Alaskan flying expedition, won fourth place, averaging 133 mph in an Orenco "D" pursuit fitted with a Wright-Hispano 300-hp engine. The Orenco was also a standard pursuit, conventional in construction, and was flown without alteration.

Fifth place went to Lt. (j.g.) A. Laverents at 125 mph in a Navy Vought VE-7 with a 180-hp Wright-Hispano engine. He far outclassed the other planes in the Vought class and so won the prize for that type.

Lt. John Roullot, USA, was sixth in a DH-4 De Havilland powered by a 400-hp Liberty engine. Averaging 124 mph, he led 12 other DH-4's in the race to win the special De Havilland class.

Following Lt. Roullot were six other DH-4's in order; then in 13th place was civilian pilot Willis Taylor in another Italian SVA, powered by a 220-hp SPA engine and similar in appearance, with the exception of W-type wing strut bracing, to the one flown by Acosta. Taylor flew at 117 mph, closely followed by Army Capt. Maxwell Kirby, who took 14th in a 180-hp Wright-Hispano engined SE-5, the only one in the race. Following the SE-5 were Vought VE-7's and De Havillands vying for the remaining places in the race; then, coming in 25th and last, was civilian Charles Colt in a French Morane-Saulnier, the only monoplane to finish the race, powered by a Le Rhone rotary engine of 110 hp, the smallest engine in the race.

U. S. Air Service Verville Scout biplane VCP-1 seen here with its Bennett race markings, top of engine cowl removed. Originally designed and flown with a 300-hp Wright-Hispano engine, this was removed and a new V-12 Packard engine of 638 hp was installed, and redesignated R-1. The original radiator was left on the aircraft, it being decided that the higher speed of the aircraft with its new big engine, would cool properly. (U. S. Air Force)

The Verville R-1 (Race No. 63) in its 1920 Pulitzer configuration and paint job. Radiator is greatly enlarged and water tank and vent placed high above the wing to prevent water from boiling out. Ducts were cut into leading edge of engine cowl top to furnish added engine cooling, exhaust stacks were streamlined with fairing that blended into engine cowling. (U. S. Air Force)

The Verville R-1 in its final configuration, as flown in the 1922 Pulizter by Captain Mosely. Seen here with engine cowling removed, the propeller spinner has been capped with a pointed cone and landing gear legs have been faired together and into fuselage with doped fabric to clean up ship. Small oil radiator air scoop has been added under fuselage just back of spinner.
(U. S. Air Force)

Designed by Grover C. Loening, this unique Wright-Martin was flown in the 1920 Pulitzer Race by Lt. B. B. Bradley, USMC, and would have finished somewhere between 1st and 4th place had he not been forced out on the very last lap with a broken water connection hose.
(U. S. Air Force)

This Curtiss 18-T Wasp triplane, powered by a new V-12 Kirkham engine of 400 hp, was one of two built in 1919 for the U. S. Navy as two-place fighter types. Both ships raced in the 1920 Pulitzer Race and proved to be quite fast but dropped out with engine trouble. Huge propeller and large radiator under center wing on fuselage side denotes high horsepower of the K-12 model engine. (U. S. Air Force)

Both Curtiss Wasp triplanes appeared at Detroit in 1922 mounted on floats and participated in the Curtiss Marine Trophy Race on October 8. This Wasp, flown by Lt. R. Irvine, USN, struck debris on the water during take-off, dropped out in the 5th lap because of excessive wind drag on the damaged portions. Lt. L. H. Sanderson, USMC, flying the sister ship, race No. 4, led the race, then ran out of fuel within sight of the finish markers. (Warren M. Bodie)

Two Navy Curtiss Wasp triplanes, each powered by a Curtiss-Kirkham V-type engine of 450 hp, started the race, but both developed engine trouble or they would probably have been up among the winners. Another interesting Navy entry was a Loening Special monoplane, which, after covering most of the course at 155–160 mph, was forced out one mile from the finish with a broken water connection; otherwise it would have finished between first and fourth.

Although the first Pulitzer race produced no record speeds, the absence of serious accidents and the highest speeds ever displayed in this country made a great impression on the spectators.

Designers, builders, and the military men left the scene with ideas for the next Pulitzer race; their competitive spirit had been thoroughly aroused and technical advancement thrives on competition.

➤   ➤   ➤

Another view of the R-1 in its 1922 Pulitzer paint job. Designed for the Engineering Division by Fred Verville, there were two VCP-1's built, one retaining its original 300-hp engine built in the U.S. by Wright under license from the French firm Hispano-Suiza. (U. S. Air Force)

This Curtiss Wasp was photographed at the St. Louis Races October 6, 1923, just after engine warm-up. Flown by Ensign D. C. Allen, USN, it crashed during the second lap of the Liberty Engine Builders Trophy Race. (U. S. Navy)

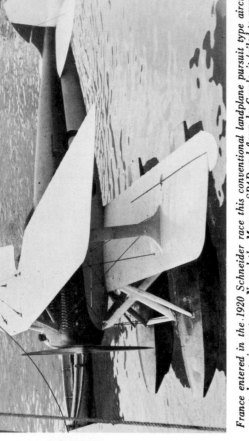
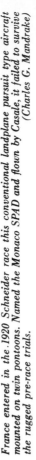

France entered in the 1920 Schneider race this conventional landplane pursuit type aircraft mounted on twin pontoons. Named the Monaco SPAD and flown by Casale, it failed to survive the rugged pre-race trials. *(Charles G. Mandrake)*

The big Macchi-19 that caught fire while flying in the 1921 Schneider, the crew of two escaping unhurt. Quite large for racing, the hydroplane, seen here with engine cowl removed, was quite fast because of its powerful 720 hp engine. *(Warren M. Bodie)*

The Savoia-13, flown by Italian pilot Ianello, became known as unofficial winner of the 1919 Schneider race, which was called off because of dense fog. Why the race was not postponed until better weather prevailed was strictly a British decision. *(Savoia-Marchetti)*

This beautifully proportioned Savoia-21, built for the 1921 Schneider, was hailed as the fastest seaplane of her time, boasted a top speed of 160 mph with her Ansaldo San Giorgio engine of 300 hp. Span of lower wing was 20', length 25'4". *(National Archives/Mandrake)*

1921 – Schneider Trophy Race

The Italian Macchi-7 flown by de Briganti, who won the 1921 Schneider with an average speed of 117.9 mph.

Held again at Venice, Italy, and over the same course as the 1920 race, the Schneider Trophy Race trials consisted of ten Italian reworked, pursuit-type flying-boat entries and one French entry. Sadi-Lecointe, the famous French speed pilot, flying a 300-hp Hispano-engined Nieuport bi-seaplane, damaged his undercarriage in alighting after a test flight and so was unable to compete.

Seven Italian entries including a Savoia S-21, the fastest seaplane of its time, were eliminated in the rugged trials, for it was a rule of the Schneider contest that only three planes be permitted to represent each country in the race.

The large number of planes dropping out during Schneider elimination trials and the races themselves, was due mostly to engine trouble — the result of constant efforts to raise engine power, mainly by higher compression and higher rpm, carried to extremes.

In the actual race, August 11, the three Italian flying boats took off separately to be timed around the course. Soon Lt. Zanetti's plane, a large Macchi-19 powered by a 720-hp Fiat 12-cyl. V-type engine, caught fire. He and his mechanic alighted and were rescued safely. Then Lt. Corniglio, flying a Macchi-7, ran out of fuel and alighted safely, leaving only de Briganti, who flew on to win the Schneider Trophy uncontested, flying his Macchi-7, with an Isotta V-type 12-cyl. water-cooled engine of 250 hp, at an average of 117.9 mph.

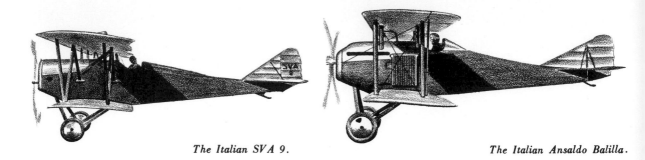

The Italian SVA 9.   *The Italian Ansaldo Balilla.*

1921 – Pulitzer Trophy Race

The second annual contest for the Pulitzer Trophy was the main attraction of an aviation meeting, held at Omaha, Neb., November 3, 4, and 5. Only six entrants appeared as against last year's large array, but the aircraft were more specialized: two were of pure race design built specifically for this race, and three were pursuit studies also built with the race in mind, leaving only one stock entrant.

Earlier this year the U. S. Navy had placed an order with the Curtiss Corporation for a special race plane that would further the development of military fighters and engines. The racer was conceived about the 1st of June, 1921; one machine was completed on August 1; another identical racer was finished August 8. These craft, the cleanest biplanes of their time, were flown early in August, with Bert Acosta as test pilot, at Curtiss Field, Mineola, L.I., and tests continued up to race time. Constructed mostly of plywood, these racers were fitted with Curtiss direct-drive CD-12 engines of 405 hp, cooled by Lamblin-type radiators fitted to the landing gear struts. When it was decided that the Navy and Army Air Services would not compete for the Pulitzer Trophy, the Curtiss Corporation requested and received the loan of one of the Navy racers for the race.

The Curtiss Corporation also designed and built a racer for oilman S. E. J. Cox of Houston, Tex., who was still anxious to get a racing aircraft into the win- column. The fuselage, engine, etc., were those of the 1920 *Cactus Kitten* monoplane now fitted with a set of triplane wings, which brought the landing speed down to about 70 mph. Tested in October by Acosta, the new Curtiss-Cox *Cactus Kitten* triplane showed a top speed of 196 mph with its Curtiss C-12 geared engine of 435 hp.

Mr. Cox had also entered in the Pulitzer his repaired Curtiss *Texas Wildcat* biplane of 1920, but this machine was ruled out because of its "unduly high" landing speed of 95.5 mph.

Italy, whose aircraft sales were world-wide because of her fine seaplanes and her stock landplanes of the first Pulitzer race, was again represented this year through the Aero Import Corporation which entered two aircraft: the Ansaldo Balilla, which had won third place in the previous Pulitzer, now fitted with a 400-hp K-12 engine as a pursuit study; and an SVA-9 two-place stock machine like that which placed 13th in the 1920 Pulitzer.

The Thomas-Morse firm of Ithaca, N. Y., anxious for more military orders, entered two single-seat fighters; one a newly designed fabric-covered parasol MB-7 monoplane; and a clip-winged MB-3 biplane, now designated an MB-6. Both were powered by Wright 400-hp V-8 engines.

On the day of the Pulitzer race, November 3, the weather was all any speed pilot could ask. The sky was clear with a bright sun, visibility was splendid, and there was but a light breeze with smooth air.

Bert Acosta won the toss-up and the privilege of starting first over the 31.07-mile triangular course, which the contestants had to cover five times. He crossed the starting line, in his new Curtiss Navy racer, at a "terrific speed" estimated at more than 200 mph and was out of sight behind the hills in a moment.

Lloyd Bertaud, in the Ansaldo Balilla, followed Acosta three minutes later. Bertaud flew high, whereas Acosta barely skimmed the line of trees on the hills.

The third pilot off was Clarence Coombs, flying the Curtiss-Cox triplane *Cactus Kitten*. When Coombs crossed the line, roaring wide open to get the very limit of speed from his red-and-silver machine, he was cheered by the spectators as their favorite. Before Coombs had got out of sight, Acosta was back, having covered the first lap in 9 min. 40 sec. He was off on the second lap before the fourth and fifth men took the air.

Harold Hartney was to follow Coombs, but be-

The Curtiss triplane CACTUS KITTEN *flown by Coombs was faster on the straightaways, while Acosta made his gains with better pylon turns in the Navy Curtiss racer and won the 1921 Pulitzer with an average speed of 176.7 mph. Note the fuselage-side radiator on the* KITTEN *and the Lamblin radiator on the Navy racer's landing gear struts. Bottom: Macready's Thomas-Morse MB-6, a modified MB-3 with shorter wings (left). The Thomas-Morse MB-7 in which Hartney crashed (right).*

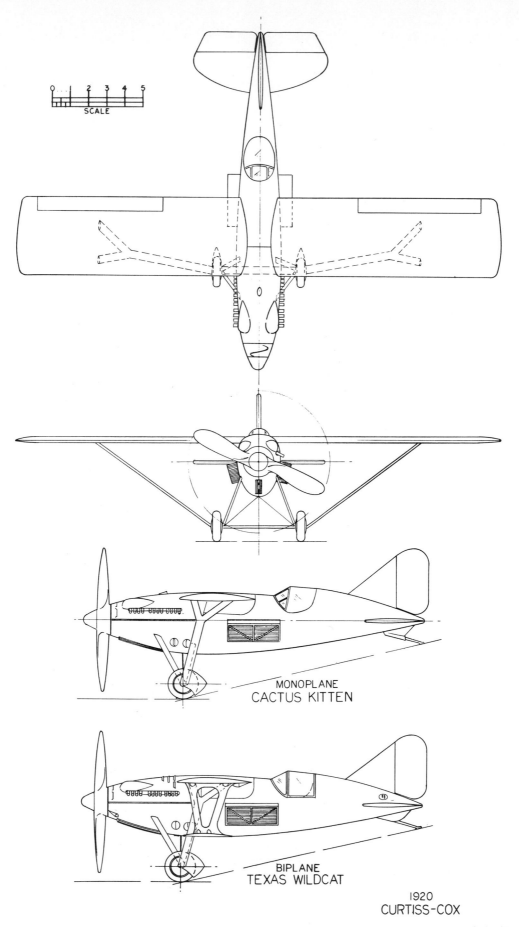

SCALE
0 1 2 3 4 5

MONOPLANE
CACTUS KITTEN

BIPLANE
TEXAS WILDCAT

1920
CURTISS-COX

D.W. CARTER 11/21/66

The Cactus Kitten triplane was composed of the fuselage, engine and other usable parts from the original monoplane *Cactus Kitten*, and a newly designed set of triplane wings of 20-foot span. After the 1921 Pulitzer, S. E. J. Cox, to whose order the Kitten was developed and raced, decided this race-plane sponsoring was getting out of hand and, in a grand gesture of patriotism, donated the Kitten to the U. S. Navy for a one dollar transfer of title fee.   (Warren M. Bodie)

Cactus Kitten, still painted red and silver but with its new owner's name painted on the vertical fin. Young Ensign Alford J. Williams, in cockpit, flew the Kitten, gathered valuable test data on the unique craft.   (Curtiss-Wright)

The Cactus Kitten as it appeared at the Curtiss factory during flight tests, and before cleanup for train shipment to Omaha for the race. Bert Acosta. Curtiss chief test pilot, in cockpit, did all initial testwork on the Kitten. *(Curtiss-Wright)*

Landing gear shock absorbers on the Curtiss racers were rubber shock cord built into the bottom of gear struts. This photo of Acosta, and the one alongside, were taken on the lawn in front of the Curtiss factory on Long Island. *(Curtiss-Wright)*

Cactus Kitten triplane had 175 sq. ft. of wing area, was quite clean in design except for the big rectangular unstreamlined brass radiators mounted on the fuselage sides. Ensign Williams poses alongside. *(Warren M. Bodie)*

Bert Acosta poses with his winning ship and the coveted Pulitzer Trophy. Acosta and Bernt Balchen later flew Adm. Richard E. Byrd and his radioman Noville across the Atlantic in a Fokker triplane to earn Byrd and Noville only the Navy DFC. *(U.S. Air Force)*

The two Navy Curtiss racers, later designated R-2 and R-3, were the cleanest biplanes built up to their time and the first to be fitted with the newly developed streamlined brace wires. Cockpit cowl is removed in side view.   (Curtiss-Wright)

The Thomas-Morse MB-6 was essentially an MB-3 pursuit ship with seven feet cut off its wing span. It was fitted with single-bay interplane struts and wore a Wright V-8 engine of 400 hp, 100 hp more than the MB-3, giving it a wing loading of slightly over 5 pounds per hp. Water cooling radiator was carried on left side of fuselage only, between wings; straightaway speed was estimated at 185 mph.
(U.S. Air Force)

cause of trouble with his gasoline pump, gave place to James Curran, in the Italian SVA-9, who was followed by J. A. Macready, flying the silver Thomas-Morse MB-6.

For the next 45 minutes the course was full of racing airplanes, as many as three coming down the straightaway at the same time.

On the third lap Curran's engine developed trouble. Forced out of the race, he made a perfect landing on the field.

From the start, the race was between Acosta and Coombs. The latter's machine, the *Cactus Kitten*, gained on straightaways, while Acosta made his gains with pylon-dusting turns. It was Coombs' first time in the strange triplane, and he wisely flew a cautious race.

Having finished his fifth lap, Acosta brought his hot-landing, little grey Curtiss biplane in smoothly, his average speed 176.7 mph, a new world speed record for a closed-course race.

Then Coombs roared over the finish line, but his time was slower, 170.3 mph, which insured second.

Macready finished in third place, averaging 160.7 mph, and then came Bertaud with 149.8 mph.

When all the other entrants had completed the course, Hartney finally took off. It was a close squeak, as the Contest Committee had given him 20 minutes in which to be off. With two minutes to spare, Hartney crossed the starting line. When 15 minutes passed and the MB-7 had not returned, anxiety became intense. Various airplanes were making ready to take off and look for him when a farmer on the course telephoned in that an airplane had crashed near Loveland, Iowa, and that the pilot was injured. Hartney was rushed to a farmhouse and treated by a physician. Although he suffered internal injuries and a fractured hip, Hartney told that his gasoline pump had failed to work, and that when he attempted to change to his reserve tank the switch stuck and he crash-landed. The Omaha Hospital later announced that Hartney was not in danger, and his recovery was expected in two months.

And so Bert Acosta, flying the Navy's beautiful little Curtiss racer, was adjudged the winner. Although he did not know it at the time, Acosta had started a chain of victories for Curtiss planes that was to place the United States in commanding lead over all nations for several years.

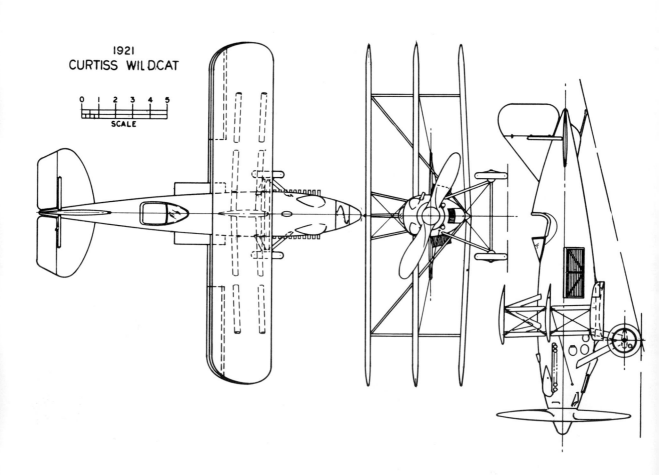

1921
CURTISS WILDCAT

0 1 2 3 4 5
SCALE

1922 – Schneider Trophy Race

England's Supermarine Sea Lion III passing Italy's Macchi-17 (center), which finished in third place, and the clean Savoia S-51 (lower right) that finished second despite a badly damaged prop. Capt. H. C. Baird, flying the Sea Lion III, won the 1922 Schneider with an average speed of 145.7 mph.

To describe in detail the 8-day aviation meet held at Naples, Italy, Sunday, August 6, to Sunday the 13th, would fill many pages. Therefore, we shall deal with only the Schneider Trophy Race, the most important event of the meet.

Held on Sunday, August 13, over a triangular course, the race was 13 laps around for a total of 200 nautical miles (230.3 statute miles). The planes, as in all Schneider races, were sent off one at a time and were clocked separately to determine the winners.

Four machines started, all flying boats with pusher-type engines, three being Italian. Capt. H. C. Baird, the lone English entry, flying a Supermarine Sea Lion III (450-hp Napier Lion engine), took off first and was followed at intervals by the three Italian ships. Capt. Baird did his first lap at more than 160 mph and held this speed for six laps, during which time he overtook and passed two of the Italian ma-

chines. From the seventh to the eleventh laps he nursed his engine a bit, and the Italian planes reduced the lead.

Then, on the 13th and last lap, Baird opened his engine and crossed the finish line, having covered the course in 1 hr. 34 min. 57.6 sec., averaging 145.7 mph, which won the trophy for England. Before alighting Baird flew two extra "insurance laps."

Passaleva of Italy, flying the cleanest entry, was handicapped early in the race when some of the laminations of his wood propeller came unstuck, setting up a terrific vibration and forcing him to throttle back. He managed, however, to fly his trim Savoia S-51 into second place averaging 143.5 mph, while third place went to Zanetti in a Macchi M-17 at 133 mph. Fourth and last place went to Cornolino in a Macchi M-7 at 90.6 mph.

❖   ❖   ❖

1922 – Pulitzer Trophy Race

General William "Billy" Mitchell, aviation leader during World War I and our greatest advocate of air power, finally convinced the stubborn land- and sea-locked Congress and military leaders of the vital necessity for aircraft development. Pointing out, among other facts, that air speeds had jumped from a 130-mph top speed in 1918 to 205 mph (France) in late 1921, solely through special racing craft, Mitchell wheedled more and more funds for experimental purposes. Spurred by orders and with ever-rising speed marks to aim for, U. S. manufacturers built the world's most advanced aircraft designs for the 1922 Pulitzer Trophy Race, held on the last day of a 3-day aviation meet near Detroit, Mich., October 12, 13, and 14. On the 12th and 13th there were the usual "class" races for various aircraft types, with but a few civilian planes appearing to compete with the military.

Just before the Pulitzer race, six Thomas-Morse MB-3 airplanes were flagged off to fly four laps, about 125 miles, over the Pulitzer course. The planes and pilots were of the First Pursuit Group, Selfridge Field, and were competing in the first annual John L. Mitchell Trophy Race, donated by Brig. Gen. "Billy" Mitchell in honor of his brother who was killed in World War I. Restricted to the First Pursuit Group, the race was won by ship No. 54 piloted by Lt. Stace at an average of 148 mph. Fine piloting was

seen in all contestants, especially at the pylons, and increased the interest in the later Pulitzer race on the part of the crowd of 25,000, who had flocked to Selfridge since early morning.

The Pulitzer course was over a circuit of 31.07 miles, which the contestants had to cover five times for a total of 155.35 miles, and was measured in kilometers for easier registry if new world's records were set. The course was mostly over the waters of Lake St. Clair: from Selfridge Field, Mount Clemens, Mich., along the shore line to Gaukler Point, then to a kite balloon anchored to a barge, thence back to Selfridge, a triangular course with roughly ten miles to a side.

At 1:00 P.M. the first four planes were flagged off into a hazy sky of moderate wind for the Pulitzer race. The contest was a free-for-all open to airplanes having an air speed greater than 140 mph and a landing speed not exceeding 75 mph. The racers were sent off in three separate groups (heats) so as to not have too many ships on the course at one time.

The first group to be flagged off in the race consisted of a Navy Thomas-Morse MB-7 similar to last year's ship (Navy Capt. Mulcahy), one Bee-Line BR-1 Navy racer (Lt. Callaway), and two Army Verville-Sperry racers.

The two Verville-Sperry planes and the Bee-Line racer wore the first retractable landing gears to be

The 1921 Navy Curtiss Racers No. 1 and 2 were both fitted with flush wing radiators, top wing only, for the 1922 Pulitzer. An additional brace strut on each side of the fuselage, which ran to the top wing between gaps in the radiator, was fitted to carry the higher loaded wing. This is Navy Curtiss No. 2 flown by Lt. Harold J. Brow. (Curtiss-Wright)

Navy Curtiss No. 2 as Lt. Brow raced it in 1922, with race No. 40 on fuselage side. Race numerals were often of a water soluble paint that could be readily washed off after racing. Later day race planes were painted well ahead of the races when possible, with numbers that were permanent, with a sleek finish that would not cause parasite drag.

(Warren M. Bodie)

Navy Lt. Brow poses in front of Navy Curtiss No. 2. Streamlining wheels with doped fabric was highly perfected by 1922, as evidenced in this view. Added strut between middle of fuselage side and wing is clearly seen, as well as skin radiator and water expansion tank atop wing.

(Curtiss-Wright)

USMC Capt. F. P. Mulcahy poses in front of Navy Curtiss No. 1 just before craft was returned to Curtiss factory for removal of Lamblin-type radiators under fuselage nose and addition of top wing skin radiator. Mulcahy was later assigned to race the Thomas-Morse MB-7 in the 1922 Pulitzer instead of this ship. *(Curtiss-Wright)*

Navy Curtiss No. 1 raced in the 1922 Pulitzer, flown by Lt. Al Williams, race No. 8 under cockpit. This ship was modified at the factory like ship No. 2. The added brace strut was placed differently in this ship, ran from top of forward landing gear strut at fuselage to just back of leading edge of wing, between gap in wing radiator. In each instance, the strut replaced a brace wire, the rear wire of ship No. 2 and the front wire on No. 1, seen here. *(Warren M. Bodie)*

Another view of Verville-Sperry R-3 A.S. 23-326, race No. 49, flown to 5th place by Army Lt. E. H. Barksdale in the 1922 Pulitzer. One of the sister ships, A.S. 23-328, which took 7th place, flown by F. B. Johnson, is parked alongside. Third R-3, article A.S. 23-327, race No. 50 (not shown) flown by Captain St. Clair Street in the Pulitzer, dropped out in the fifth lap with a frozen engine. All three craft were painted olive drab overall except for markings. Hangars in background are Selfridge Field, Mt. Clemens, Mich. *(U. S. Air Force Museum)*

Three Verville-Sperry R-3 racers, designed by Alfred Verville and built at the Sperry plant, were procured by the Army Air Service for the 1922 Pulitzer race. All three ships wore Lamblin-type water radiators slung under their wing at the center and were fitted with retractable landing gear, with no wheel-well covers provided, thus causing undue drag. Ships were built as pursuit studies and needed only leak-proof gas tanks to convert them. *(U. S. Air Force)*

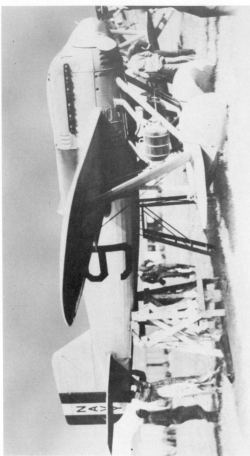

Combined drag of the many and long struts of the landing gear, plus its twin Lamblin radiators, presented tremendous drag on the N-W1 aircraft. Tail stand was necessary for access to engine and propeller for hand cranking.

(*Warren M. Bodie*)

Trim little Gloster Mars 1 won the English Aerial Derby race in 1921-22 and set an official world speed record of 212.15 mph on October 4, 1922. Nicknamed "Bamel" by her crew, this well-proportioned ship was powered by a 450 hp Napier Lion engine.

(*Gloster*)

The Navy NW-1 Mystery was the first aircraft to wear full wheel pants and attracted a lot of attention because of its unusual design.

(*Dustin W. Carter*)

Air Service serial No. A.S. 6856, Curtiss R-6 racer designation and procurement number P-278 are clearly visible in this side view of Lt. Maitland's ship. The fuselage, struts, stabilizer and fin of both R-6 racers were painted a dull black.

(*U.S. Air Force*)

Two Navy-Wright sesquiplane racers were built in 1922 as flying test beds for a new 650-hp V-12 Packard T-2 engine. Designated NW-1, the first of the two ships, nicknamed "Mystery" (above), was completed in time for the 1922 Pulitzer. Racer No. 9, Navy serial A-6543, was dunked and turned over in four feet of Lake St. Clair water when its engine failed. USMC pilot Lt. Sandy Sanderson was barely able to scramble through bottom muck and swim ashore.   (U. S. Navy)

The second Navy-Wright NW-1 aircraft, A-6544 above, did not race but carried on its duties as an engine test bed. This craft was later rebuilt as a twin-float bi-seaplane, entered by the Navy in the 1923 Schneider race, and designated an NW-2.
(U. S. Navy)

Streamlined water expansion tank mounted atop fuselage in front of the cockpit of the Bee Line racers, acted as a wind screen in lieu of a transparent shield. Sister ship, BR-2, is seen in background, over rudder of BR-1. *(U.S. Air Force Museum)*

Army Lt. D. F. Stace, winner of the 1922 John L. Mitchell Race, standing alongside his trim little MB-3 pursuit in which he averaged 148 mph. *(U.S. Air Force)*

Navy Lt. Callaway awaits a crank for his BR-1 on the race starting line. Oil radiator is seen under fuselage at wing leading edge root. None of the aircraft at the 1922 race meet were fitted with wheel brakes, still depending on tail skid to stop. *(U.S. Air Force)*

In design theory the R-4 was supposed to be rugged in construction and the thick wing was to give the ship good take-off and landing characteristics. The big bore 600 hp Packard engine was, hopefully, to pull it through the air at good speed. *(U.S. Air Force Museum)*

The Navy ordered two Bee Line low-wing monoplane racers for the 1922 Pulitzer race and they were identical except for their radiators. One, the BR-1, was fitted with flush-type radiators built into the top of the wing surface and the sister ship, the BR-2, wore a Lamblin-type radiator on each side of its fuselage at the wing root. Above ship was flown in Pulitzer by Navy Lt. Callaway.   (U.S. Navy/Bodie)

Navy Lt. Rittenhouse in front of the BR-2 which did not race because of mechanical trouble. The Bee Line aircraft were designed by Booth and Thurston of the Aerial Engineering Corp. of Hammondsport, N.Y., an outfit newly formed by ex-Curtiss employees.   (U.S. Air Force Museum)

publicly demonstrated in the United States. The cold mention of this fact does little justice to the emotion the onlookers felt when the three pilots actually did crank their landing gears into the fuselage.

The Navy Bee-Line racer designed by Booth and Thurston, former Curtiss engineers, who had worked on the 1921 Navy Curtiss racers, was not sufficiently flight tested before the races, but in design was the most promising of all, with many new ideas that were to survive the race. Powered by a Wright H-3 engine of 380 hp, the entire wing was covered with a thin sheet of copper, under which the cooling water circulated so that the copper acted as a radiator as well as wing structure. The retractable landing-gear legs wore full skirts, so when the wheels retracted into the wing the wheel wells were completely covered.

The Verville-Sperry planes were pursuit studies, powered by 380-hp Wright H-3 engines. They were full cantilever in construction and very clean, except that the wheel wells were uncovered, certainly causing quite a lot of air drag.

The story of this race was brief, for the Bee-Line racer dropped out in the second lap due to radiator trouble, and the Navy Thomas-Morse MB-7 followed suit with lubrication trouble. This left only the two Verville-Sperry ships, and both finished, Lt. Barksdale making an average speed of 181 mph and Lt. Johnson 178 mph, which was good for only fifth and seventh places in the final results.

The second group of Pulitzer racers sent off was comprised of two new Army Curtiss biplane racers, two identical Navy Curtiss biplane racers, one of which had won first place in the 1921 Pulitzer, plus a Navy "Mystery" ship. The latter had been completed only shortly before the race, and its hurried assembling and testing handicapped its chances.

The Navy "Mystery" racer was built as a flying test bed for a new 650-hp Packard T-2 engine, the most powerful of its day. A sesquiplane of unusual appearance, her pilot, Lt. Sanderson, reported her to be admirably controllable and most satisfactory to fly.

The Curtiss racers, and in particular the two clean Army ships, were naturally the favorites, for it was known that Lt. Maughan in one of these ships had attained in unofficial tests at Garden City, N. Y., a speed of 222 mph, a new record. The question most discussed was whether these fast ships would prove maneuverable enough on the turns to hold the speed they would make on the straightaways.

Despite the "terrific" speed of their ships, the Army's Lt. Maughan and Lt. Maitland swung them around in perfect banks at the pylons with no more visible difficulty than the standard pursuit ships had

had a few hours previously. Lt. Maughan was banking his turns at least 80° and clearing the pylons by a few feet.

Lt. Sanderson handled the brand-new Navy "Mystery" plane like a veteran, cutting the pylons even a bit sharper than Maughan. He made one lap at 187 mph but was forced out in the fourth lap by engine trouble, setting the "Mystery" down in water at 90 mph and swimming ashore uninjured. Sanderson seemed pursued by ill luck, for he had a week previously lost what seemed to be a sure victory in the Curtiss Marine Trophy Race (restricted to Navy service types), when his Curtiss triplane ran out of gas while within sight of the finish line.

Lt. Maughan broke all world's records for speed in a closed circuit for 100 and 200 km to win the heat, averaging 205.8 mph. Lt. L. J. Maitland, flying a sister ship to Maughan's Curtiss, finished second with an average of 198.8 mph, and Navy Lt. Brow was third with his Curtiss R-2 averaging 193.2 mph.

Lt. Alford Williams, in the fourth Curtiss racer, the Navy R-1, had a thrilling experience when a fire extinguisher in his cockpit exploded, a piece of it knocking his helmet off. He had great difficulty arranging his helmet while plunging on at better than three miles a minute, and though fumes from the extinguisher sickened him, he succeeded in finishing fourth at 188 mph. Speeds of the four Curtiss racers proved to be the fastest of the day, winning first, second, third, and fourth places in the race.

Lt. Maughan was exhausted by the race and leaned against his plane for a few minutes until he had revived. "I got lost four times in the haze," Maughan said. "I was stunned (blacked out) more or less at each of the fifteen turns. On the straightaway I came to. Another trouble I had was with my feet going to sleep." We know today that Maughan was making his turns too abruptly — it was estimated that he was pulling at least 7G's (seven times gravity) in his turns!

The last group of Pulitzer racers, which was sent off at 3:46 P.M., was comprised of the Verville-Packard VCP-1 biplane, with which Capt. Mosely won the 1920 Pulitzer race, and which he again piloted in this year's race; two new Army Loening low-wing racers, piloted by Lts. Whitehead and Schulz; two Army Thomas-Morse TM-22 raised-wing (parasol) monoplanes, piloted by Capt. Hunter and Lt. Bissell; and the third remaining low-wing Verville-Sperry with retractable gear, piloted by Capt. St. Clair Streett.

The Loening racers were powered by new 600-hp V-12 Packard engines, but were handicapped by thick wings and a fixed and not very streamlined

Both MB-7 aircraft wore a 320-hp Wright V-8 engine in a shapely fuselage but were handicapped by a weird wing that sat too close to the fuselage. Top speed was estimated to be 180 mph, landing speed 80. Capt. F. P. Mulcahy, USMC, who piloted the MB-7 in Pulitzer, poses above.
(U. S. Navy)

Another homely product of the Thomas-Morse Aircraft Corp. was this MB-7 fabric-covered parasol monoplane, two of which were hopefully built in 1921 for possible sale as pursuit studies. Only one was finished in time for the 1921 Pulitzer and ex-military pilot Harold Hartney cracked it up in a forced landing during the race. The second MB-7, above, was purchased by the Navy for the 1922 Pulitzer.
(U. S. Air Force)

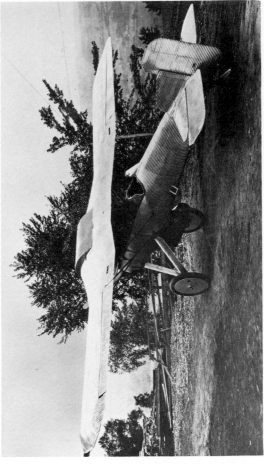

Nieuport-Delage full-cantilever sesquiplane was built for the 1922 Deutsch de la Meurthe Cup Race. Windshield and headrest of open cockpit can be seen above the wing. Engine is a 380 hp Hispano V-8.
(U.S. Air Force)

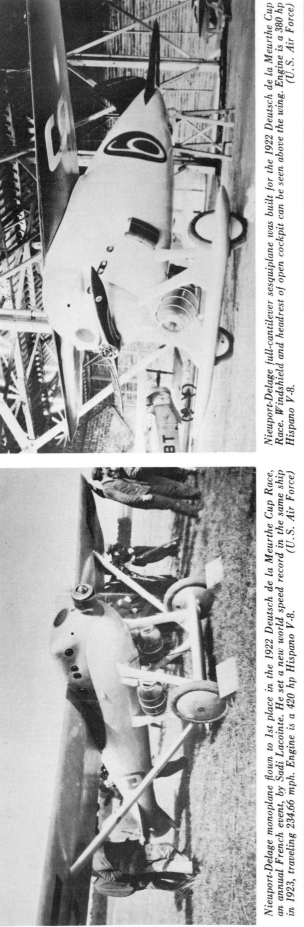

Nieuport-Delage monoplane flown to 1st place in the 1922 Deutsch de la Meurthe Cup Race, an annual French event, by Sadi Lacointe. He set a new world speed record in the same ship in 1923, traveling 234.66 mph. Engine is a 420 hp Hispano V-8.
(U.S. Air Force)

One of the two TM-22 R-5 racers sitting on a ridge near the Thomas-Morse factory at Ithaca, N.Y. Fuel tank was fitted into wing at the middle. The wing itself was built into two panels, left and right, and had no center section.
(U.S. Air Force)

Landing gear of the R-4 was rugged, with big wheels for rough field operation, such as pursuit ship might encounter in normal operation. Landing brace wire running from wheel outside center to wing prevented wing vibration on Whitehead's ship.
(U.S. Air Force)

Two Loening R-4 low-wing monoplanes with fixed landing gears, designed as pursuit studies, were built for the 1922 Pulitzer in 60 days before race time. Lt. Ennis Whitehead test flew the R-4 (race No. 46) that he was to pilot in the Pulitzer and reported that at full speed the wing tips vibrated at least two feet vertically and he was sure they would come off. Radiator area also proved inadequate so the fuselage back of the engine was faired and both ships were flown minus cowls.

(U. S. Air Force)

With the race only a few days off there was no time to build new wings for the R-4 racers, so a dedicated crew worked around the clock giving the wings torsional strength by veneer covering in the case of Lt. Whitehead's plane, and external struts (above) on Lt. Schultz's craft (race No. 45). Both R-4's were condemned after the race, almost total flops.

(Warren M. Bodie)

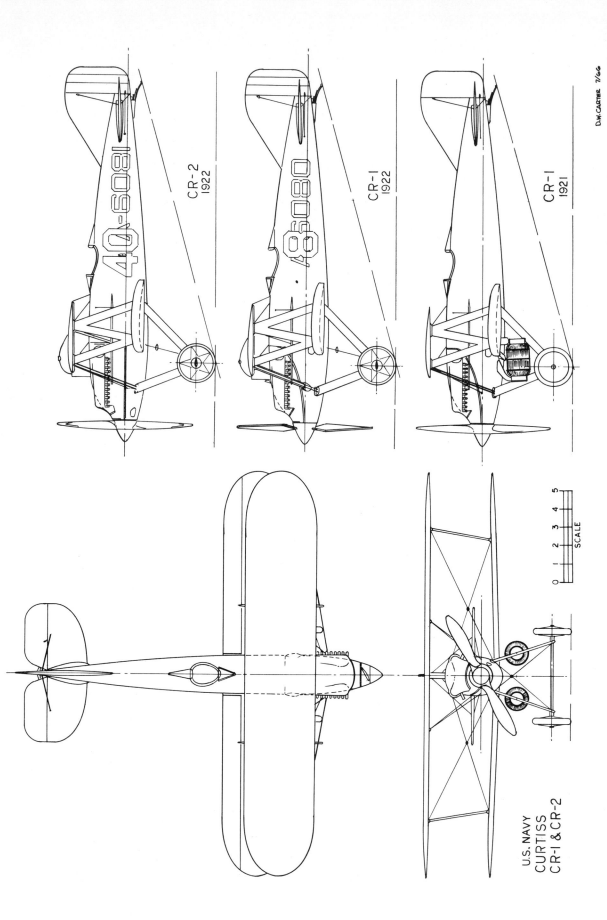

CR-2
1922

CR-1
1922

CR-1
1921

D.W.CARTER 7/66

SCALE
0 1 2 3 4 5

U.S. NAVY
CURTISS
CR-1 & CR-2

The exquisite CR-2, later identified as model R-6, is considered by many Curtiss racer fans to be the most beautiful aircraft ever built. Two were built under contract No. 552, dated May 27, 1922, between the Army and Curtiss. Contract required a sea level top speed of 175 mph, and landing speed not over 75 mph. The craft bore procurement Nos. 278 and 279. Lt. Russell L. Maughan poses with R-6 No. 2, P-279, in which he won Pulitzer. (Curtiss-Wright)

Army Lt. L. J. Maitland poses with CR-2 No. 1 (P-278) in which he finished second in the Pulitzer. Both CR-2 aircraft were re-worked during the winter, and between March 21 and 29, 1923, new speed trials were made at McCook Field, Dayton, Ohio. Racer No. 2 (P-279) established a new record of 236.598 mph. In September both ships were plagued by mishaps and did not do well in the October 1923 Pulitzer despite new and more powerful engines. (Curtiss-Wright)

Denied sufficient funds for purchase of research aircraft, Air Services frequently bought racing craft under the guise of pursuit studies. Two Thomas-Morse TM-22 parasol monoplanes similar to model above, were acquired in 1922 and designated R-5 racers. Homely in appearance, it was ahead of its time in having all-metal construction and wore a big Packard V-12 engine of 600 hp in a clean fuselage but was handicapped by an awkward and thick wing.   (U. S. Air Force)

A thick wing section was used on the R-5's in an effort to give the aircraft shorter take-off and landing rolls, plus good climb—desirable characteristics for pursuit ships. Several propellers were tried on the TM-22's. the one above used on No. 48 necessitated an almost 3-point take-off because of its length.
(Warren M. Bodie)

landing gear, which held the planes' speed down.

The three Thomas-Morse planes, two Army TM-22's and one MB-7, were specially built by the Ithaco firm for the race and were very similar to the MB-7 of last year's race. The TM-22 racers were entirely of metal construction, covered with corrugated sheet aluminum. The TM-22's were powered by 12-cyl. Packard engines of 600 hp, and the MB-7 wore a 380-hp Wright H-3.

In contrast with speeds of the previous racers, it was at once apparent that none of these ships could make the time of the Curtiss racers. The old Verville-Packard, piloted by Mosely, made the best time of this group, averaging 179 mph to take sixth place in the race. (Lt. Barksdale having won fifth place in the first heat.)

Capt. Streett, after doing the fourth lap at 169 mph, developed engine trouble on the fifth and last lap and landed safely just outside Selfridge Field.

Lt. Whitehead and Lt. Schulz, in their Packard-engined Loenings, took second and third in the heat and eighth and ninth places in the race, averaging 170.2 and 160.9 mph respectively. Then came Lt. Bissell and Capt. Hunter in their TM-22's, to finish in the last places in the heat and the race. Capt. Hunter, unfortunately, got lost in the haze on the first lap and wasted about five minutes, but thereafter made better time than two of those who were credited with finishing ahead of him.

When the last ship had landed, and the timers' stand announced the victory of Lt. Maughan, a great volume of cheers broke out, for the victory had placed America in the front rank of military aviation.

Four days later, amplifying his plea for air power development through racing craft, Gen. "Billy" Mitchell flew the winning Curtiss plane four runs over a 3-km course, averaging 224.4 mph to break the world's speed record.

The four Curtiss racers, particularly the two Army Curtiss planes, still hold title as being the most beautiful and streamlined biplanes ever built, as well as the fastest for their power. The success of these craft was to cause U. S. pursuit and fighter planes to be predominantly biplane through the 20's and into the 30's.

The two Army Curtiss planes were faster than the Navy's, for they were designed from knowledge gleaned in building and flying the two Navy racers.

Designed and built in but 90 days, the Army Curtiss planes were the first to have oil and water radiators built into the wings. Curtiss designed, they were made of corrugated brass and were the ultimate in streamline cooling for water-cooled engines.

The wings, fuselage, and fixed tail sections were constructed of wood, then plywood covered; the ailerons, elevators, and rudder of metal, then fabric covered. The engine cowling was metal. The Army Curtiss planes were of shorter span than the Navy's, had I interplane struts instead of the Navy's N type, and were powered by Curtiss V-12 engines (D-12) of 460 hp.

The Navy Curtiss planes were further streamlined for this year's race and had wing radiators (top wing only) instead of the old Lamblin type.

◆   ◆   ◆

Direct front view of the Thomas-Morse TM-22 (R-5). Water-coolant radiator suspended under fuselage was encased in a metal shell in an effort to streamline it.
(U. S. Air Force/Bodie)

1923 – Schneider Trophy Race

Though the Schneider races had contributed little to technical progress, they had increased interest in aviation. The entries from 1919 to 1922 had been reworked single-seat pursuit seaplanes. From 1913 to 1922 the Schneider races had remained a field of activity for the sportsman pilot and the aircraft manufacturer. Technical development was slow and systematic preparation at a minimum until the respective governments took an active interest in the races.

Pure racing craft appeared in the 1923 Schneider, when the United States was represented by a full team for the first time. The team, entered by the U. S. Navy, consisted of four pilots: Lt. David Rittenhouse and Lt. Rutledge Irvine, both flying float versions of the Navy's two Curtiss racers (465-hp D-12 engines) of 1921-22 Pulitzer fame; Lt. Frank Wead, whose biplane Navy Wright NW-2 seaplane, powered by a Wright T-3 700-hp engine, was eliminated before the trials by a broken propeller blade which ripped open the floats and caused the machine to crash on alighting; and Lt. A. W. Gorton, flying a TR-3A biplane, the reworked Navy TR-1 in which he had won first place in the Curtiss Marine Trophy Race in 1922.

The TR-3A was fitted with wing radiators and a 265-hp Wright water-cooled engine in place of its regular 200-hp radial air-cooled Wright. This plane was entered as an alternate and was used by the U. S. pilots to familiarize themselves with the racecourse.

The British Schneider Cup team originally consisted of three planes, but two of them were crashed by their pilots during tests, leaving only H. C. Baird to fly a Supermarine Sea Lion III flying boat with a Napier Lion engine. This plane was the same that won the Schneider Cup in 1922 at Naples, Italy, but the engine was boosted to 575 hp, new wings were fitted, and the design was cleaned up.

The French team consisted of four biplane machines; two CAMS flying boats, each with a 360-hp Hispano-Suiza engine; and two Latham LI flying boats, each with two 400-hp Lorraine-Dietrich tandem-pusher and tractor engines.

The CAMS boats differed in that the CAMS 36 had a tractor propeller, while the CAMS 38, fitted with a pusher prop, was 10 mph the faster of the two.

The two Latham flying boats were the French "bad weather" chance, of very sturdy construction, and would have made a showing only on a windy day with choppy water. One of these was so damaged by shore helpers that it had to be withdrawn.

Large crowds watched the qualifying tests held the day before the race. Each machine was required to taxi over the starting line, take off and alight three times, and then lie at anchor unattended for six hours.

These provisions called for a rugged and seaworthy plane, and the American machines, being pontoon type, were watched with much interest, as it was believed that they would "porpoise." They behaved well, however, taxiing fast and getting off quickly.

The race proper was held on Friday, September 28, over the triangular Cowes-Selsey-Southsea course, which measured 42.86 statute miles, five times around for a total distance of 214 miles. The weather was fine, with bright sunshine and calm sea, though the wind freshened later.

At 11:00 A.M. the starting signal was given to Lt. Irvine, who quickly left his spray path behind and took-off in his sleek grey Navy Curtiss. He was soon followed by his teammate Lt. Rittenhouse in the other Curtiss, but engine trouble prevented the third plane of the American team, the TR-3A, from starting.

Fifteen minutes later and just as Lt. Irvine roared by to finish his first lap, Baird of England, in his Supermarine, crossed the starting line. Then the start was given to the three French machines, but only the fastest one, the CAMS 38 piloted by M. Hurel, crossed the starting line. The CAMS 36 fouled a mooring buoy on its take-off run, while the Latham did not get away at all because of trouble with its tandem engines.

The two Curtiss ships streaked by, to be followed by the Supermarine. Hurel developed engine trouble early in the second lap and alighted off Selsey, his speed for the first lap but 130.4 mph.

It was soon evident that the U. S. Curtiss planes were much faster than England's fastest entry, and that, barring engine trouble, the Cup would go to the United States.

And so it did. Rittenhouse worked up to first place and finished with an average speed of 177.4 mph. Lt. Irvine finished second with 173.5 mph, and Baird, in the Supermarine, secured third place with 157.2 mph. Then Lt. Rittenhouse roared around the course once more on his "insurance" lap and was clocked at a new high of 188.2 mph for seaplanes.

It was a great day for American aviation. For the first time an American plane and engine flown by an American pilot had won the famous Schneider.

The British and French paid warm tribute to the efficiency of the American team and said the Curtiss planes were the cleanest and most perfect racing

Both U. S. Navy Curtiss racers of 1921-22 Pulitzer fame (A-6080 and A-6081) were fitted with twin pontoons for entry in the 1923 Schneider Trophy race. Additional weight was carried by new Curtiss D-12 engines delivering 450 hp at 2300 rpm. Designations were changed again. In 1921 the ships were CR-1, in 1922 CR-2 and now were CR-3 as seaplanes. Both photos on this page are of CR-3 A-6081, with Lt. David Rittenhouse, Schneider winner, in cockpit.   (Curtiss-Wright)

Several changes were visible in the Curtiss racers as seaplanes. Struts were substituted for the remaining double-brace wires that ran from inboard section of the top wing to the lower fuselage. Wing radiators were added outboard of the N struts on the top wing to cool the larger engines, and the newly developed Curtiss-Reed metal propellers were installed on both craft. Fuel tanks were placd in the floats, a feature to be much copied abroad.   (Curtiss-Wright/Brodie)

The rather large and awkward Navy-Wright NW-2 which was a rebuild of the 1922 Navy-Wright NW-1 sesquiplane. Craft suffered a pre-race accident so did not race. All four Navy racers went to England by cruiser in 1923.

(Curtiss-Wright)

This unique and promising English entry, a Blackburn "Pellet," G-EBHF race No. 6, powered by a 450 hp Napier Lion engine, crashed before the 1923 Schneider race. Lamblin radiator and oversize wing tip floats were its only poor features.

(Charles G. Mandrake)

Interesting TR-3A bi-seaplane was re-worked Navy TR-1 which had won the 1922 Curtiss Marine Trophy race for service craft. Plane went to England in 1923 as an alternate and was used by the U.S. team for practice.

(U.S. Navy)

The Supermarine Sea Lion III flying boat of 1923 was a re-work of the 1922 Schneider winner cleaned up and wearing a new big engine of 575 hp. It was designed for seaworthiness, had struts and wires galore.

(U.S. Navy)

aircraft yet seen in Europe. Of special interest to them were the Curtiss-Reed metal propellers on the Curtiss racers (the first metal props ever flown) and the wing radiators of all our entries.

Partly through increased horsepower, but mainly by its use of wing radiators and metal prop, the winning Curtiss traveled faster as a seaplane than the same ship had in winning the 1921 Pulitzer when fitted with wheels.

◆   ◆   ◆

The Curtiss racers, foreground and upper left, finished easily in first and second place over England's Supermarine Sea Lion III (upper right). Lt. Rittenhouse, No. 4, worked up to first place and set a new speed record for seaplanes, winning the 1923 Schneider race with an average speed of 177.4 mph. Bottom: The TR-3A, reworked Thomas-Morse Navy Scout (left). The 700-hp Navy Wright NW-2, damaged by broken prop, crashed (second from left). The French CAMS 36 fouled a mooring buoy on take-off (second from right). The French Latham (right).

Direct rear view of the Curtiss R2C-1, photographed on September 9, 1923, shows wing skin radiators on both wings, fabric covered ailerons and elevators.

(Curtiss-Wright)

1923 – Pulitzer Trophy Race

The St. Louis Air Meet, held October 4, 5, and 6, was by far the biggest and best aeronautical demonstration in the world up to this time, with 125,000 persons witnessing the last day's events. Over 300,000 miles were flown without a serious accident. To describe the whole meet would require a volume in itself, and so we will stick to the most important event, the Pulitzer Trophy Race, which did so much to develop our nation's military and racing aircraft.

Held on the last day of the meet, the Pulitzer Trophy Race was comprised of seven highly developed racing craft, all of them constructed mainly of wood, with plywood-covered wings and fuselages and the movable surfaces fabric .covered. Water-cooled engines and wing radiators were installed on all seven planes. The Navy had spent a lot of money on monoplanes for last year's race, only to see biplanes take the first four places. Justly believing biplanes more suitable for her newly converted carrier, the U.S.S. *Langley*, and anxious to win over the Army, she placed her bets on a proven builder by ordering two new and improved Curtiss biplanes (R2C-1) for this race. Perfectly streamlined, they differed from previous Curtiss racers in that their fuselages were smaller, the top wings were flush with the fuselage, and the landing gear simplified. Powered by Curtiss D-12 Special engines of 500 hp, both planes wore the newly invented Curtiss-Reed metal propellers, which had been proven in the Schneider race eight days earlier.

In an effort to exploit biplanes to their fullest, the Navy also ordered two biplane racers from the Wright Company. Although powered by Wright T-3 engines of 700 hp, the highest horsepower in the world at this time, the Wright F2W racers were poor copies of the Curtiss racers and not as clean in streamline.

The Army Air Service spent little money this year on its Pulitzer entries. Two of them were the Curtiss ships which took first and second in last year's race, one even having the same engine, while the other had the new 500-hp D-12 Special engine. A third Army entry, the Verville-Sperry, the low-wing monoplane which had flown in the 1922 race (see illustration on page 53) now fitted with a 500-hp D-12 Special engine, was the only monoplane of the race.

To reduce possibilities of accident, it was decided, as in past Pulitzer races, to pair the contestants and run the race in heats over the 124.28-mile 4-lap course.

THE FIRST HEAT

Lt. Lawson "Sandy" Sanderson of the Marines was first into the clear blue sky with his red Navy Wright. He did a climbing turn over the field beyond the starting point and, after reaching 4,000 feet, swung far into the sun and then dived straight for the first pylon. He flashed by the timers at 2:31 P.M. and, rounding the pylon, left a smoky trail in the eastern horizon as he streaked out of sight.

Only one of the original three Verville-Sperry R-2 (A.S. 22-328) appeared at St. Louis for the 1923 Pulitzer race. Fitted with a special D-12 engine of 500 hp, it wore a new streamlined engine cowl complementing its enlarged propeller spinner. Spinner nose cone became loose, setting up a vibration that forced Lt. Alex Pearson to drop out in the first lap. The R-3, with full cantilever low-wing configuration and retractable landing gear, was ahead of its time. (U. S. Air Force)

The elegantly beautiful Curtiss R2C-1 racers of 1923 were the epitome of biplane streamlining, had only one main landing gear leg on each side and used streamline wires from the axles as side braces to absorb extra loads. Above is A-6691 with Lt. Harold J. Brow in the cockpit. This ship was first test-flown by Lt. Brow with a wooden propeller while its sister ship wore one of S. Albert Reed's forged one-piece duraluminum props from the first. (Curtiss-Wright)

As in the R-6 Curtiss racers, the R2C (with Lt. Williams) had a semi-monocoque wood fuselage with "Curtiss ply" 2-ply spruce veneer, glued and tacked in strips two inches wide diagonally to the frame, fabric covered, doped and waxed to a high lustre. Entire water supply, about 12 gallons, was circulated through the wing radiator, top and bottom wings, over five times a minute. Radiator skin was fabricated with corrugated brass sheet of only .004" thickness. (U.S. Air Force)

Lt. Sanderson alongside his F2W which wore a 3-bladed wooden propeller in the Pulitzer. Sling with wooden pole handles over fuselage just forward of vertical stabilizer was used by ground crew to hold tail skid in its dolly when moving aircraft about.

(U.S. Navy)

R2C-1 A-6692 in which Lt. Alford J. Williams won the 1923 Pulitzer race. Design of the two R2C's was largely the work of Curtiss' chief engineer William L. Gilmore, who created all the Curtiss racing craft, from the Wildcat to the R3C-1 of 1925. Power loading of the R2C-1, only 4.17 lbs/hp, gave the ships a then fantastic climb to 5,000 feet in 1.6 minutes, 10,000 feet in 3.6 minutes, 15,000 feet in 5.8 minutes and 20,900 feet in 10 minutes. *(U. S. Air Force)*

The two 1923 Navy Wright F2W racers were practically enlarged copies of the Curtiss R-6 Army racers of 1922 fame, their larger size necessary to handle the huge 700-hp V-12 Wright T-3 Tornado engines fitted to both ships. On the rudder of both F2W aircraft were the words "NAVY WRIGHT FIGHTER" to justify their purchase to a penny-pinching Congress. No. 8, above, was test-flown with a two-bladed propeller, raced with the three-bladed one. *(U. S. Navy)*

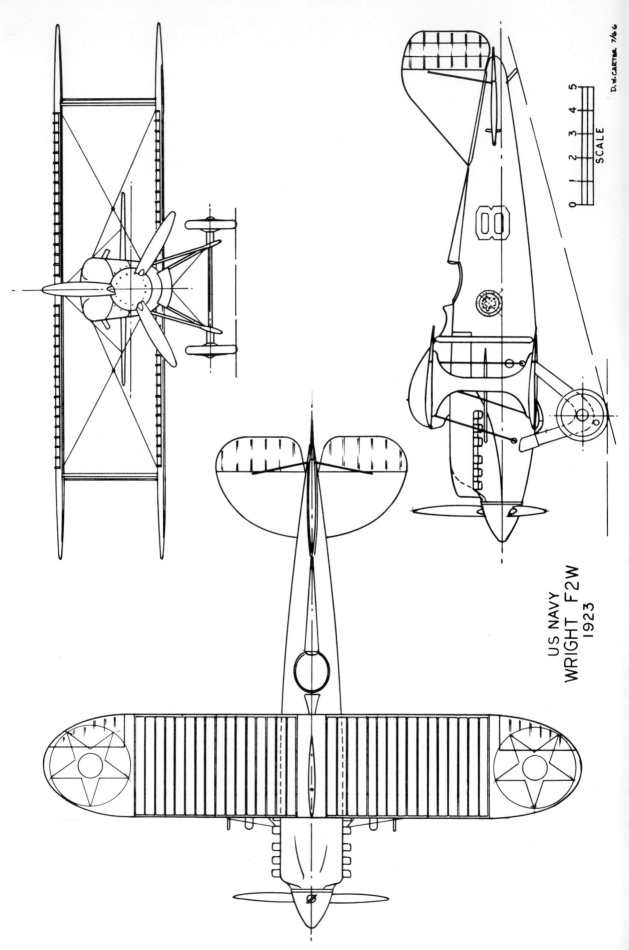

D.W. CARTER 7/66

SCALE
0 1 2 3 4 5

US NAVY
WRIGHT F2W
1923

Although seen here with a three-bladed propeller, F2W No. 7 was flown in the 1923 Pulitzer with a two-bladed propeller —and both ships finished only seconds apart in the Pulitzer. (Warren M. Bodie)

Navy Wright F2W-1 as it rolled out of the factory for initial test flights, and before being final-painted with fire engine red fuselage, white wings and tail surfaces. Fuselage of the F2W was unique in that its entire length was built up of wood, then plywood and fabric covered, the only metal being in its motor mount and the top front of the fuselage which streamlined the cylinder banks. (Curtiss-Wright)

Lt. Harold Brow took R2C-1 A-6691 on its first test flight at Mitchell Field on September 9, 1923, and four days later piloted this ship to 244.3 mph in level flight to set an unofficial first in exceeding four miles per minute. *(U.S. Air Force)*

Lt. L. Sanderson, USMC, in his Navy Wright F2W No. 8 awaiting starter's flag for Pulitzer Race, October 6, 1923. *(U.S. Navy)*

Although larger than the earlier R-6 racers, the R2C-1 was still quite small as view shows, with Lt. Williams alongside. Aileron and empennage control surfaces had metal frames and doped linen covering. No control cables or horns protruding. *(Curtiss/Bodie)*

Navy Lt. S. W. Callaway taking off in his Navy Wright F2W No. 7 for a practice flight just before race day. *(U.S. Navy)*

Sharp, revealing view of the 1923 modified Verville-Sperry R-3 shows, over its tail, a Fokker XCO-4 and DH-4 aircraft in the background that flew in the then annual Liberty Engine Builders Trophy Race. (U.S. Air Force Museum)

Just before race time the Verville-Sperry R-3 was fitted with wheel-well covers that had been made earlier. This view was taken just after the R-3 had dropped out of the Pulitzer. Note missing spinner nose cone. (U.S. Navy)

Lt. Lawson H. M. (Sandy) Sanderson, USMC, left, poses with Lt. S. W. Calloway, USN, alongside Calloway's F2W just before race time. Note two-bladed propeller. Neither F2W wore transparent windshields but were fitted with half-conical windbreaks in front of cockpit. (U. S. Navy)

One of the Navy Wright F2W ships as it left the Wright factory for delivery to Navy where it would receive its red and white paint job, complete to insignia and race number. Large size of F2W is seen here as aircraft seems to dwarf its pilot. (U. S. Navy)

A moment later Lt. Corkill took off in the black Army Curtiss racer. He made a steep dive on the pylon from 3,000 feet, turning it so closely that there were doubts as to whether he went around it, but the judges ruled the race on.

Soon Lt. Sanderson was swinging wide around the home pylon to turn in 240.3 mph for his first and fastest lap, and then Corkill, a bit off course, flew by at a 210 mph clip. Corkill was troubled by loose glasses in his goggles, and the earth "seemed to quiver" until finally, on the third lap, he succeeded in readjusting them and picked up speed. His plane, fitted with a crash pad but with no windshield to protect him, flew at such speed that the wind stripped the top of his leather helmet off. Corkill whirled around the triangular course to average 216.5 mph for the race, not enough to overcome the steady pounding of his Marine opponent, who finished well ahead with an average speed of 230.1 mph.

Zooming over the finish line, Sanderson climbed to 2,000 feet like a rocket, his luck finally allowing him to finish a race. His luck gave out just then though, for in his gliding turn around the field his gas tank went dry, and he disappeared behind a railroad embankment in a fast glide. Seeing a soft haystack, Sandy headed for it. The crash came and when Sandy came to, his first thought was to get clear of the wreck before it burned. He felt quickly for his safety belt and then, brushing the straw from his eyes, found that he was far from his mangled ship but still strapped to his seat, and was wearing a new collar — the leather cockpit ring! Sandy had suffered only a sprained ankle and abrasions on his face and hands.

THE SECOND HEAT

Lt. Al Williams took off in his new blue R2C-1 Navy Curtiss racer, with an engine bark that was loud beyond belief and, after his climbing turn, dived past the starting line with a whine like that of a high explosive shell. The terrific roar of a D-12 engine, either in a climb, level flight, or dive, has never been equaled to this day.

Then Lt. Pearson took off, climbed, and dived across the starting line in his slate-colored Army R-3 Verville-Sperry. But the low-wing monoplane didn't get a chance to prove its worth, for hardly had Pearson reached the far end of the field when he was forced to turn back and land. The propeller spinner had come loose, unbalancing the prop and setting up a terrific vibration.

And now Williams was roaring over the timers' stand at 245.3 mph, a mark unprecedented in the annals of aviation.

THE THIRD HEAT

With Pearson out, the third and last heat was flagged off with Williams still in the air. Lt. S. Callaway, in the red Navy Wright racer, took off first, followed by Lt. H. J. Brow in the blue Navy Curtiss, a sister ship to Williams' racer, trailed by Lt. W. Miller in the black Army Curtiss racer, a twin ship to Corkill's racer.

Williams, meanwhile, had been flying his beautiful little Curtiss around the course with exact precision and finished the race with an average speed of 243.7 mph.

It then remained to be seen whether Williams' time could be beaten by the three pilots entered in the last heat. It was not, and Lt. Al Williams had set new speed records for the 100- and 200-km distances, and had bettered last year's winning speed by more than 37 mph.

Navy Lt. Brow finished second with 241.8 mph, and all six planes exceeded last year's record. America was leading the way for all future aircraft design!

In November, Lts. Williams and Brow engaged at Mitchel Field, N. Y., in dive starts from thousands of feet in the air, flying their Curtiss racers low over a 3-km course in competition for the world's speed record. This contest ended with the speed mark being raised by Lt. Williams to 266.6 mph on November 4, when the Secretary of War called a halt to their dramatic but extremely dangerous duel.

Lt. Calloway making his start in the Pulitzer race.   (U. S. Navy)

Wing load is in lbs. per sq. ft. throughout

JAMES GORDON BENNETT CUP 1909–1920

YEAR	COURSE and PLACE		PILOT	NATION	RACE NO.	AIRCRAFT	ENGINE (w) water-cooled	HP	SPAN	LENGTH	EMPTY	GROSS	WING LOAD	AV. SPEED	REMARKS
1909	2 laps—12.43 mi. Rheims, France	1	Glenn Curtis	U.S.	8	Curtis Golden Flyer	Curtis V-8 (w)	50	26'3"	25'	470	690	3	47.65	Pusher type. Level top 60 mph.
		2	Louis Bleriot	France	22	Bleriot XI	E.N.V. V-8 (w)	60	31'2"	25'	510	720	4.5	46.83	Tractor type.
		3	Hubert Latham	France	13	Antoinette	Antoinette V-8 (w)	50	46'	27'10"	990	1200	3.03	42.5	Tractor type.
		4	Eugene Lefebvre	France	2	Wright	Wright 4 cyl. (w)	25	41'	40'	750	1100	2.05	35.7	Level top speed 52 mph.
			Cockburn	England		H. Farman	Gnome rotary 7 cyl.	35	32'6"	39'	975	1212	3		Level top speed 37 mph.
1910	20 laps—62.137 mi. Belmont Park, Long Island	1	Grahame-White	England		Bleriot XI bis	Gnome 14 cyl. 2 row	100	23'9"	26'6"	530	750	5.76	61	Crashed 19th lap. 1 lap 71 mph.
		2	Moisant	U.S.		Bleriot XI	Gnome rotary 7 cyl.	50	28'2"	26'6"	510	720	4.5	31.5	
		3	Alec Ogilvie	England		Wright "C"	Wright 4 cyl. (w)	35	38'	29'9"	800	1150	2.63	29.4	Landed for 54 min.
		4	Hubert Latham	France		Antoinette	Antoinette V-16 (w)	100	49'3"	43'	1050	1350	3.33	17.8	Landed for 4 hrs.
			Leblanc	France		Bleriot	Gnome 14 cyl. 2 row	100	23'9"	26'6"	530	750	5.76		
			Drexel	U.S.		Bleriot XI	Gnome rotary 7 cyl.	50	28'2"	26'6"	510	720	4.5		Out 8th lap, engine trouble.
			J. Radley	England		Bleriot XI bis	Gnome 14 cyl. 2 row	100	23'9"	26'6"	530	750	5.76		Out 2nd lap, engine trouble.
			Walter Brookins	U.S.		Baby Wright racer	Wright V-8 (w)	50	21'5"	24'	685	860	5.92		Stalled on take-off, crashed.
1911	25 laps—94 mi. Eastchurch, Eng.	1	Chas. Weymann	U.S.		Nieuport	Gnome 7 cyl.	100	27'6"	23'	700	925	5.3	78	
		2	A. Leblanc	France		Bleriot	Gnome 7 cyl.	100	16'6"	26'6"	750	948	6.2	75.83	
		3	M. Nieuport	France		Nieuport	Gnome 7 cyl.	70	27'6"	23'	700	890	4.9	75.07	
		4	Alec Ogilvie	England		Baby Wright	N.E.C. V-8 (w)	50	21'5"	24'	685	860	5.92	53.31	
			M. Chevalier	France	12	Nieuport	Nieuport 7 cyl.	28	27'6"	23'	520	740			Out 12th lap. Av. 48 mph.
			Hamel	England	4	Bleriot	Gnome rotary 7 cyl.	100	17'	26'6"	750	948	6.2		Crashed on 1st turn.
1912	30 laps—124.8 mi. Chicago, Ill.	1	Jules Vedrines	France		Deperdussin	All entries	160	19'6"	21'	710	1040	11.7	105.5	Fastest laps 107 mph.
		2	Prevost	France		Deperdussin	Gnome 14-cyl. 2 row	100	23'	20'6"	700	1030	10.3	103.8	Out 24th lap. Av. 94.3 mph.
			Andre Frey	France		Hanriot	Air-cooled rotary	100							
1913	20 laps—124.3 mi. Rheims, France	1	Prevost	France	1	Deperdussin	All entries	160	19'6"	20'	992	1411	10.24	124.5	Fastest lap 127 mph.
		2	Emile Vedrines	France	5	Ponnier		160	23'	17'	1006	1425	9.89	123	Fastest lap 125.5 mph.
		3	Gilbert	France	2	Deperdussin	Gnome 14-cyl. 2 row	160	21'10"	20'	1001	1421	10.1	119.5	
		4	Crombez	Belgium	17	Deperdussin	Air-cooled rotary	160	21'10"	20'	1001	1421	10.1	106.9	
1920	3 laps—186.4 mi. Etampes, France	1	Sadi-Lecointe	France	10	Nieuport	Hispano-Suiza V-8	320	19'6"	20'3"	1521	2060	15.6	168.5	All engines in this race water-cooled.
		2	Bernard de Romanet	France	8	Spad	Hispano-Suiza V-8	320	28'6"	21'9"	1950	2875	10.5	113.5	Landed once. 1st lap 162 mph.
			Kirch	France	11	Nieuport	Hispano-Suiza V-8	320	19'6"	20'3"	1521	2060	15.6		Out 3rd lap. 1st lap 181.5 mph.
			Raynham	England	4	Martinsyde Semiquaver	Hispano-Suiza V-8	320	20'2"	19'3"		2025	6.7		Out 2nd lap. Broken oil pump.
			Maj. R. W. Schroeder	U.S.	1	Verville-Packard	Packard V-12	638	28'2"	24'2"	2485	3233	14.12		Out 1st lap. VCP-1.
			Howard Rinehart	U.S.	2	Dayton-Wright	Hall-Scott 6 cyl.	250	21'	22'8"	1400	1850	18		Top speed 200 mph. Out 1st lap.
			Roland Rohlfs	U.S.	3	Curtis *Texas Wildcat*	Curtis C-12 V-12	435	26'	19'3"		2300	25.5		Top speed 215 mph. Pre-race crash.

SCHNEIDER TROPHY RACE 1913–1931

Wing load is in lbs. per sq. ft. throughout

YEAR	COURSE and PLACE	#	PILOT	NATION	RACE NO.	AIRCRAFT	ENGINE	HP	SPAN	LENGTH	EMPTY	GROSS	WING LOAD	AV. SPEED	REMARKS
1913	Monaco — 28 laps—174 mi.	1	Prevost	France	19	Deperdussin	Gnome 14 cyl. twin	160	44'3"		2095	2646	8.8	45.75	Av. 60 mph.—reflew marker.
			Weymann	U.S.	6	Nieuport	row, all entries	160	39'7"	28'7"	1323	1874	7.27		Out 5th lap. Av. 68.8 mph.
1914	Monaco — 28 laps—174 mi.	1	C. H. Pixton	England	3	Sopwith Tabloid	Gnome 9 cyl. rotary	100	24'7"		992	1433	5.7	86.75	
		2	Burri	Switzerland	7	F.B.A.	both entries	100			1323	1874	9.2	62	
1920	Venice, Italy — 10 laps—222 mi.	1	Lt. Luigi Bologna	Italy	7	Savoia S-12	Ansaldo V-12	500	36'5"			4784	20.62	107.2	Only contestant—bad weather.
1921	Venice, Italy — 10 laps—222 mi.	1	Lt. Briganti	Italy	1	Macchi M-7	Isotta V-12	250	32'8"		1720	2382	9.4	117.859	Only ship of 3 to finish.
			Lt. Zanetti	Italy	2	Macchi M-19	Fiat V-12	720	51'7"		5489	6150			Forced out, fire. Did 141 mph.
1922	Naples, Italy — 13 laps—230.3 mi.	1	Capt. H. C. Baird	England	1	Supermarine Sea Lion III	Napier Lion V-12	450	31'10"	27'6"	2381	3163	9	145.7	Fastest entry—prop vibration.
		2	Passaleva	Italy	2	Savoia S-51	Itala (Hispano) V-12	300	32'9"	26'1"	1716	2376	9.2	143.5	
		3	Zanetti	Italy	3	Macchi M-17	Isotta V-12	250						133	
		4	Cornolino	Italy	4	Macchi M-7	Isotta V-12	250						90.6	
1923	Cowes, England — 5 laps—214 mi.	1	Lt. D. Rittenhouse	U.S.	4	Curtiss R-3 Navy	Curtiss D-12 V-12	465	22'8"	25'	2119	2747	16.35	177.38	1 lap 188.17 mph, seaplane record.
		2	Lt. R. Irvine	U.S.	8	Curtiss R-3 Navy	Curtiss D-12 V-12	465	22'8"	25'	2119	2747	16.35	173.46	Sister ship to winner.
		3	Capt. H. C. Baird	England	7	Supermarine Sea Lion III	Napier Lion V-12	575	32'	27'6"	2403	3240	9.24	157.17	Reworked 1922 Sea Lion II.
			M. Hurel	France	10	CAMS 38	Hispano-Suiza V-12	360	28'2"	25'5"	1675	3200	10.2		Out 2nd lap. 1st lap 130.4 mph.
			Lt. Frank Wead	U.S.		Navy Wright NW-2	Wright T-3 V-12	700	28'	28'5"		4447	16.7		Damaged floats—crashed in trial.
1925	Baltimore, Md. — 7 laps—217.49 mi.	1	Lt. James Doolittle	U.S.	3	Army Curtiss R3C-2	Curtiss V-1400	619	22'	20'2"	2028	2738	19.04	232.573	Set 4 records. 3 km 245.713 mph.
		2	Capt. Hubert Broad	England	5	Gloster III	Napier Lion VII	700	20'		2028	2650	18	199.169	Fastest lap 201.536 mph.
		3	G. de Briganti	Italy	7	Macchi M-33	Curtiss D-12	435	32'	27'4"	2073	2777	17	168.444	Fastest lap 173.858 mph.
			Lt. George Cuddihy	U.S.	2	Navy Curtiss R3C-2	Curtiss V-1400	619	22'	20'2"		2738	19.04		Out 7th lap.
			Lt. Ralph Ofstie	U.S.	6	Navy Curtiss R3C-2	Curtiss V-1400	619	22'	20'2"		2738	19.04		Out 7th lap.
			Capt. H. C. Baird	England	4	Supermarine S-4	Napier Lion VII D	675	30'6"	27'	2425	3150	23.1		Crashed in trials. 226.6 mph.
1926	Hampton Roads, Va. — 7 laps—217.49 mi.	1	Maj. de Bernardi	Italy	5	Macchi M-39	Fiat A.S. II V-12	800	30'4"	22'1"	2760	3263	22.52	246.496	1 lap 248.520 mph.
		2	Lt. Christian Schilt	U.S.	6	Curtiss R3C-2	Curtiss V-1400	619	22'	20'2"	2050	2738	19.04	231.363	1 lap 233.164 mph. Same as 1925.
		3	Lt. Bacula	Italy	3	Macchi M-39	Fiat A.S. II V-12	800	30'4"	22'1"	2760	3263	22.52	218.006	Sister ship to winner.
		4	Lt. T. Tomlinson	U.S.	4	Curtiss F6C-1 Navy	Curtiss D-12	435	22'					136.953	
			Lt. Geo. Cuddihy	U.S.		Curtiss R3C-4 Navy	Curtiss V-1570	700	22'	20'					Out 7th lap. 1 lap 242.16 mph.
1927	Venice, Italy — 7 laps—217.49 mi.	1	Flt. Lt. S. N. Webster	England	6	Supermarine S-5	Napier Lion VII G	875	26'9"		2536	3197	27.85	281.65	Record 319.5 mph Nov. 4, 1928.
		2	Flt. Lt. O. F. Worsley	England	4	Supermarine S-5	Napier Lion VII D	875	26'9"		2602	3043	26.62	273.07	
			Capt. Guazzetti	Italy	7	Macchi M-52	Fiat A.S. III V-12	1030	28'10"			3439	27.99		Out 6th lap. Record 318.4 mph March, 1928.
			Flt. Lt. S. M. Kinkead	England	1	Gloster IV B	Napier VII G	875	22'8"	26'4"	2415	3085	22.19		Out 4th lap. 1 lap 277.14 mph.
			Maj. de Bernardi	Italy	5	Macchi M-52	Fiat A.S. III V-12	1030	29'5"			3160	23.9		Out 2nd lap.

YEAR	COURSE AND PLACE		PILOT	AIRCRAFT	COUNTRY	ENGINE	HP	No.	SPAN	LENGTH	EMPTY	GROSS	WING LOAD	AV. SPEED	REMARKS
1929	Cowes, England 7 laps—217.49 mi.	1	Flt. Off. Waghorn	Supermarine S-6	England	Rolls-Royce R V-12	1920	2	30'	28'8"	4471	5250	36.2	328.63	Full wt. 5771 lbs. Wing load 39.8.
		2	Qtrmstr. T. Dal Molin	Macchi M-52R	Italy	Fiat A.S. III V-12	1030		25'9"			3263	29.69	284.20	1927 model. One lap 287.78.
		3	Flt. Lt. d'Arcy Greig	Supermarine S-5	England	Napier Lion VII G	875		26'9"		2536	3197	27.85	282.11	World record 1928.
			Flt. Off. R. Atcherley	Supermarine S-6	England	Rolls-Royce R V-12	1920	4	30'	28 8"	4471	5250	36.2		Cut pylon. Rec. 100 km 331.75, 50 km 332.49.
			Lt. Remo Cadringher	Macchi M-67	Italy	Isotta-Fraschini V-18	1400	7	29'6"			4740	32.8		Out 2nd lap. 1st lap 283.88.
			Monti	Macchi M-67	Italy	Isotta-Fraschini V-18	1400	10	29'6"			4740	32.8		Out 2nd lap. 1st lap 301.47.
1931	Lee on Solent, England 7 laps—217.49 mi.	1	Lt. J. H. Boothman	Supermarine S-6B	England	Rolls-Royce Buzzard V-12	2350		30	28'10"	4590	6086	41.3	340.1	Record 405.997 mph Sept. 29, 1931, by Lt. Stainforth in a S-68. The engine developed more than 2600 hp.

PULITZER TROPHY RACE 1920–1925

YEAR	COURSE AND PLACE		PILOT	RACE NO.	AIRCRAFT	ENGINE Air-cooled (a)	HP	SPAN	LENGTH	EMPTY	GROSS	WING LOAD	AV. SPEED	REMARKS
1920	4 laps—116.08 mi. Mitchel Field, Long Island	1	Capt. Corliss Mosely	63	Verville-Packard	Packard 1A-2025, V-12	638	28'2"	24'2"	2485	3233	14.12	156.5	186 mph. Normal top.
		2	Harold E. Hartney		Thomas-Morse MB-3	Wright-Hispano V-8	300	26'	19'11"	1360	2037	8.1	148	171.25 mph. Normal top.
		3	Bert Acosta		Italian SVA A-1	SPA 6 cyl. in-line	220	25'	21'8"	1470	1965	8.7	134.5	147 mph. Normal top. Balilla.
		4	Lt. St. Clair Streett		Orenco "D"	Wright-Hispano V-8	300	30'	21'6"	1666	2432	9.3	133	147 mph. Normal top.
		5	Lt. A. Laverents		Vought VE-7	Wright-Hispano V-8	180	34'1"	24'5"	1560	2100	7.35	125	
		6	Lt. John Roullot	16	De Haviland DH-4	Liberty V-12	400	42'6"	21'11"	2390	3600	8.2	124	DH-4's placed 6th to 12th.
		13	Willis Taylor		Italian SVA 9	SPA 6 cyl. in-line	220	22'11"	19'8"	1600	2144	8.5	117	
		14	Capt. Maxwell Kirby		SE-5A	Wright-Hispano V-8	180	26'9"	20'10"	1570	2060	8.7	116.7	DH-4's and VE-7's placed 15th to 24th.
		25	Charles Colt		Morane-Saulnier	LeRhone rotary (a)	110	28'7"	18'8"		1155	12.5	95	Pursuit trainer.
			Lt. B. G. Bradley, USMC	46	Loening Special	Wright-Hispano V-8	300	30'5"	24'2"	1450	1850	12.5	150	Out last lap.
1921	5 laps—155.35 mi. Omaha, Nebraska	1	Bert Acosta		Navy Curtiss R-1	Curtiss CD-12	405	22'8"	21'	1735	2165	12.5	176.7	Straight top 200 mph. New
		2	Clarence Coombs	3	Curtiss-Cox	Curtiss C-12	435	20'	19'3"	1936	2406	13.75	170.26	1920 Cactus Kitten fuselage.
		3	J. A. Macready		Thomas-Morse MB-6	Wright V-8	400	19'	18'6"	1512	2023	12.3	160.71	Army R-2 racer.
		4	Lloyd Bertaud		Ansaldo Balilla	Curtiss K-12, V-12	400	26'	22'6"	1823	2367	10.5	149.78	1920 reworked New eng., 4 blade prop.
			Harold E. Hartney		Thomas-Morse MB-7	Wright V-8	400	24'	18'6"	1502	1975	17.6		Crashed 1st lap. Straight top 179 mph.
			James Curran		Italia SVA-9	SPA 6 cyl. in-line	220	22'11"	19'8"	1600	2144	8.5		Out 3rd lap. Engine trouble.
1922	5 laps—155.35 mi. Detroit, Michigan	1	Lt. R. Maughan	43	Army Curtiss R-6	Curtiss CD-12	460	19'	18'11"	1454	1950	14.1	205.8	Best lap 207 mph. New
		2	Lt. L. J. Maitland	42	Army Curtiss R-6	Curtiss CD-12	460	19'	18'11"	1454	1950	14.1	198.8	Best lap 203 mph. New
		3	Lt. H. J. Brow	40	Navy Curtiss R-2	Curtiss CD-12	405	22'8"	21'	1735	2165	12.5	193.2	Best lap 196 mph. Built 1921.
		4	Lt. Alford Williams	8	Navy Curtiss R-1	Curtiss CD-12	405	22'8"	21'	1735	2165	12.5	188	Best lap 190 mph. Winner 1921.
		5	Lt. E. H. Barksdale	49	Verville-Sperry R-3	Wright H-3, V-8	380	32'4"	22'5"	1795	2225	14.83	181	Normal top 191 mph. Low-mono. New
		6	Capt. Corliss Mosely	42	Verville-Packard R-1	Packard 1A-2025, V-12	638	27'6"	24'7"	2763	3511	15.04	179	Reworked 1920 winner.
		7	Lt. F. B. Johnson	48	Verville-Sperry R-3	Wright H-3, V-8	380	32'4"	22'5"	1795	2225	14.83	178	
		8	Lt. E. C. Whitehead	45	Loening R-4	Packard 1A-2025, V-12	600	27'	21'	2102	2700	15.5	170.2	Condemned after race. Wing flutter. New
		9	Lt. L. D. Schulz	46	Loening R-4	Packard 1A-2025, V-12	600	27'	21'	2102	2700	15.5	160.9	Condemned after race. Low-mono. New

YEAR	COURSE and PLACE		PILOT	RACE NO.	AIRCRAFT	ENGINE Air-cooled (a)	HP	SPAN	LENGTH	EMPTY	GROSS	WING LOAD	AV. SPEED	REMARKS
1923	4 laps—124.28 mi.	1	Lt. Alford Williams	9	Navy Curtiss R2C-1	Curtiss D-12 Spl., V-12	500	22'	19'8"	1565	2071	14	243.67	Best lap 245.27 mph. New
	St. Louis, Missouri	2	Lt. H. J. Brow	10	Navy Curtiss R2C-1	Curtiss D-12 Spl., V-12	500	22'	19'8"	1565	2071	14	241.78	Sister ship to winner. New
		3	Lt. L. H. Sanderson, USMC	8	Navy Wright F2W	Wright T-3, V-12	700	22'6"	21'4"	2420	3000	17.2	230.06	Top 240.3 mph. New
		4	Lt. S. W. Callaway	7	Navy Wright F2W	Wright T-3, V-12	700	22'6"	21'4"	2420	3000	17.2	230	New
		5	Lt. W. Miller	49	Army Curtiss R-6	Curtiss D-12 Spl., V-12	500	19'	18'11"	1465	1961	14.2	218.91	Winner 1922. New engine.
		6	Lt. J. D. Corkill	50	Army Curtiss R-6	Curtiss D-12, V-12	460	19'	18'11"	1454	1950	14.1	216.45	Took 2nd 1922.
			Lt. A. Pearson	48	Verville-Sperry R-3	Curtiss D-12 Spl., V-12	500	30'6"	23'5"	1950	2475	16.9		Out 1st lap. Spinner loose. 1922
1924	4 laps—124.28 mi.	1	Lt. H. H. Mills	70	Verville-Sperry R-3	Curtiss D-12 Spl., V-12	500	30'6"	23'5"	1955	2475	16.9	215.72	Raced 1922-23.
	Dayton, Ohio	2	Lt. W. H. Brookley	69	Army Curtiss R-6	Curtiss D-12 Spl., V-12	500	19'	18'11"	1465	1961	14.2	214.75	Winner 1922.
		3	Lt. Rex Stoner		Curtiss Hawk PW-8A	Curtiss D-12, V-12	460	30'	22'2"	1986	2819	11.05	167.95	
			Capt. Burt Skeel		Army Curtiss R-6	Curtiss D-12 Spl., V-12	500	19'	18'11"	1465	1961	14.2		Crash dived. Ship placed 2nd 1922.
1925	4 laps—124.28 mi.	1	Lt. Cyrus Bettis	43	Army Curtiss R3C-1	Curtiss V-1400, V-12	619	21'9"	19'10"	1792	2182	15.1	248.975	New joint Army-Navy design.
	Mitchel Field,	2	Lt. Alford Williams		Navy Curtiss R3C-1	Curtiss V-1400, V-12	619	21'9"	19'10"	1792	2182	15.1	241.695	New joint Army-Navy design.
	Long Island	3	Lt. Dawson		Curtiss Hawk P-1	Curtiss V-1150-1, V-12	435	31'6"	22'6"	2041	2841	11.36	169.9	New production pursuit. Taperwing.
	(Last Pulitzer Race)	4	Lt. Norton	50	Curtiss Hawk PW-8	Curtiss D-12, V-12	460	32'	22'10"	1865	2761	10.4	168.8	Production pursuit.
		5	Capt. Cook		Curtiss Hawk PW-8	Curtiss D-12, V-12	460	32'	22'10"	1865	2761	10.4	167.4	
			Lt. C. T. Cuddihy		Curtiss Hawk PW-8	Curtiss D-12, V-12	460	32'	22'10"	1865	2761	10.4		Out 4th lap, engine.

Index